AF226054

POISE & POSE

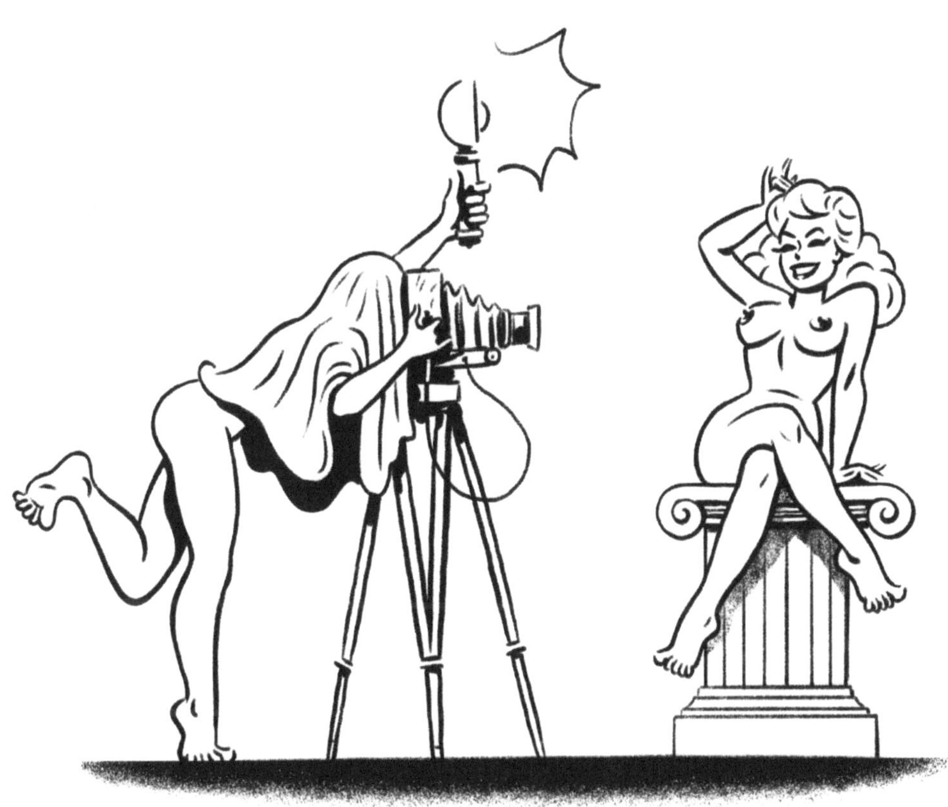

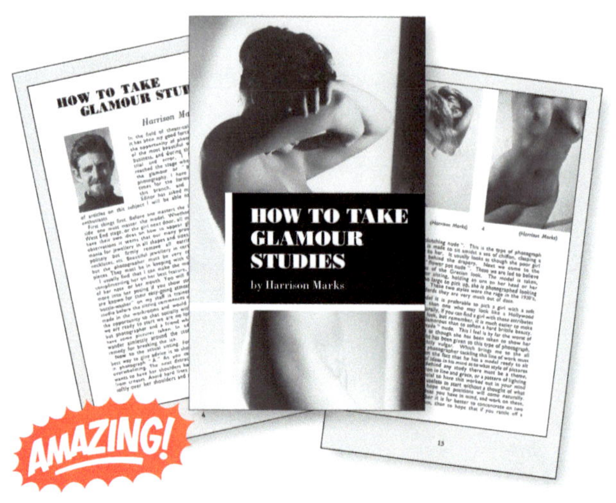

Receive a **FREE** copy of
How to take Glamour Studies by Harrison Marks
when you sign up to our mailing list at
www.pamela-green.com/mailing-list

Published in 2021 by Wolfbait Books © 2021

www.wolfbait.co.uk

ISBN: 978-1-9162151-4-6

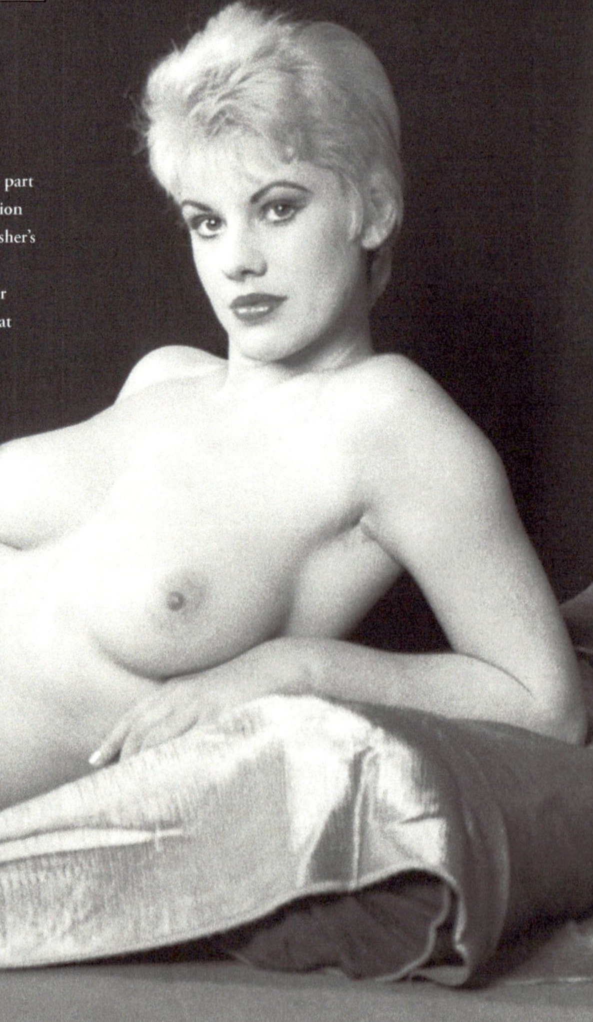

POISE & POSE

By Yahya El-Droubie

Photography by Stephen Glass

Illustrations by Colin Gordon

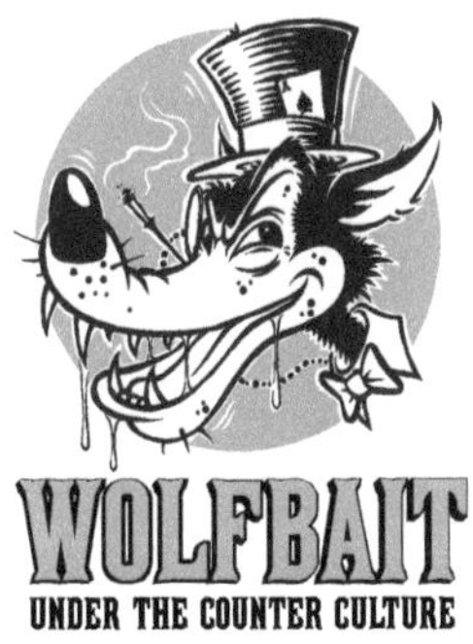

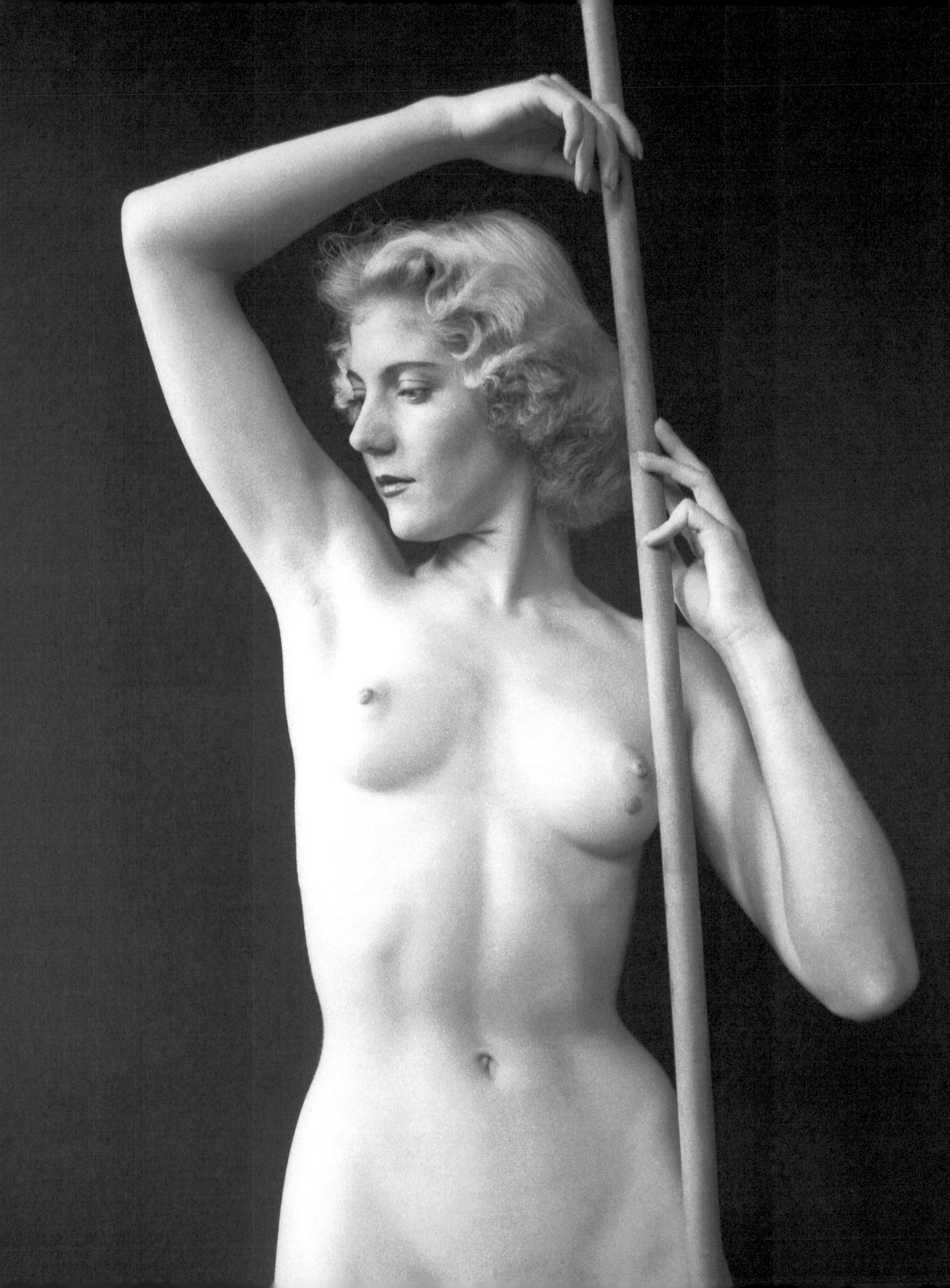

Introduction

THE HUNGARIAN PHOTOGRAPHER Stephen Glass is something of an enigma. During the 1950s his name was sufficiently well-known to be displayed prominently on magazine covers as a sales tool, but almost nothing was written about him or his work at that time. The opposite is true of his younger brother, Zoltán, who was also a photographer. Known to his friends as "Zolly", he was featured and interviewed in many magazines on both sides of the Atlantic.

History has recorded little about the Glass brothers' parents, Rezno and Olga, or about the boys' early years, but what is known is that following three years of intensive study at commercial art schools in Budapest, Stephen earned a living as a designer, cartoonist, and painter. Zoltán was born in Budapest on April 26, 1903 and, following in his brother's footsteps, began his career as an artist and caricaturist. He struggled to make ends meet, however, and took various other jobs to supplement his income, among them docker, night watchman, photographic retoucher, and stage designer. Apparently, he even dabbled in a spot of acting. In 1925, Zoltán moved to Berlin, Germany, where, like his brother, he was employed as a picture editor at an evening newspaper.

As members of a network of talented Hungarian émigrés, the Glass brothers prospered. In 1930 Zoltán established Reclaphot, a photographic agency that specialised in advertising work, and Autophot, a company dedicated exclusively to automobile photography. The brothers would often work together. A keen motorsports enthusiast and amateur racer, Zoltán covered Germany's biggest races at the Nürburgring and Avus circuits. His most famous photographs are of the Mercedes-Benz Silver Arrows team, which dominated Grand Prix racing during the mid-1930s.

By 1936 doing business in Germany was becoming increasingly difficult for the brothers, who were Jewish, and they fled to London. Zoltán was given work by another Jewish refugee, Arthur Spingarn, the owner of Sackville Advertising;

— Sir Kenneth Clark

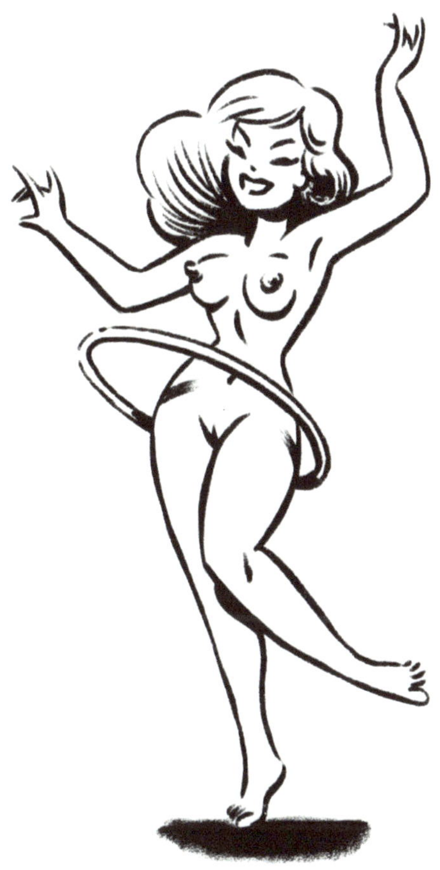

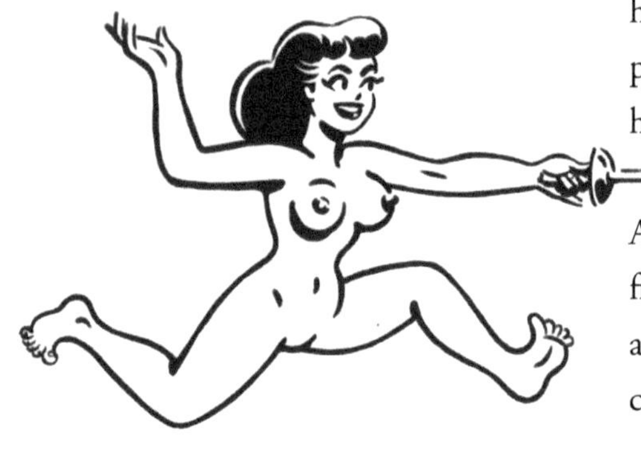

however, as an enemy alien at the outbreak of World War II in 1938, he was not permitted to pursue his profession and faced the threat of internment. As a result, he voluntarily handed over his camera equipment to the British authorities.

After the war, Zoltán eked out a living taking publicity stills for clients in the film and theatre worlds. In 1948, after twelve years as an émigré, he became a naturalised British subject. It was around this time that Stephen began to concentrate on naturist photography.

Zoltán's career took a big step up when fellow Hungarian Arpad Elfer, creative director at Colman, Prentis and Varley, one of the most prestigious London advertising agencies, started giving him work. By the mid-1950s, he was one of the most successful fashion and advertising photographers in the capital, with a studio at 183 Kings Road, Chelsea, and later, another at 41 Paradise Walk, SW3.

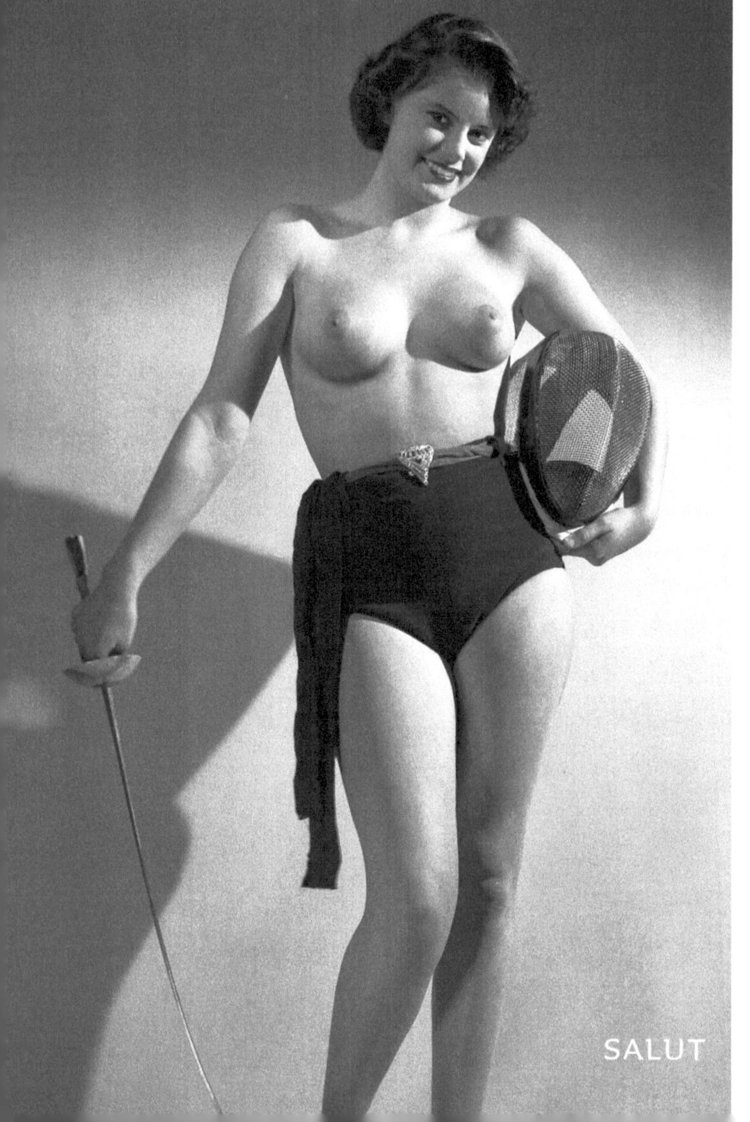

SALUT

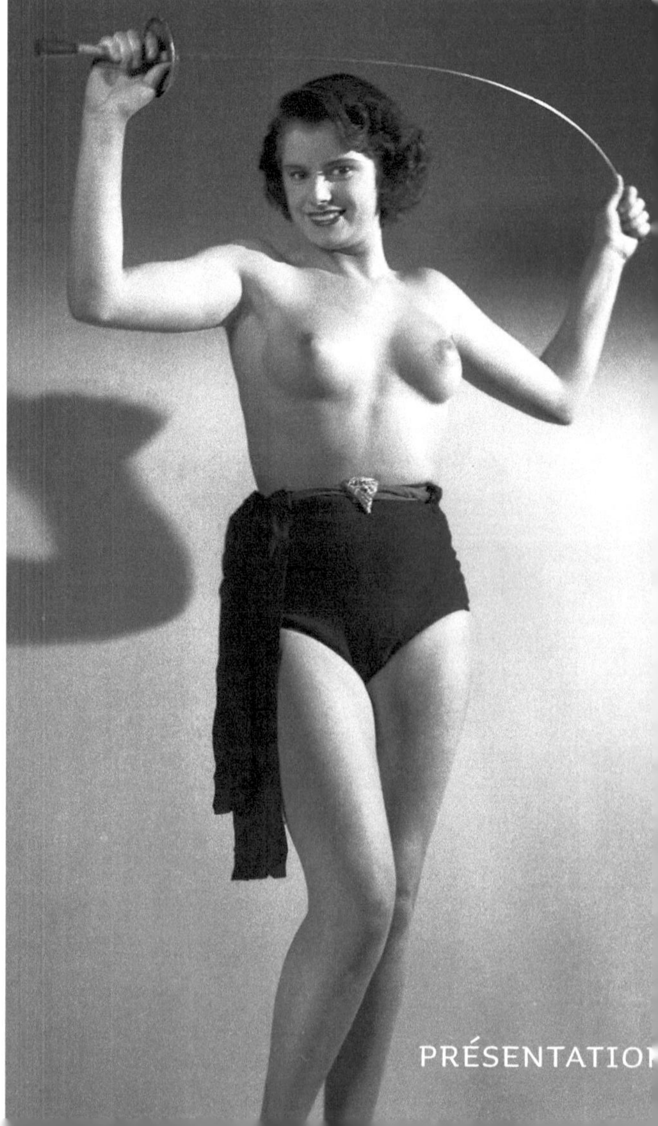

PRÉSENTATION

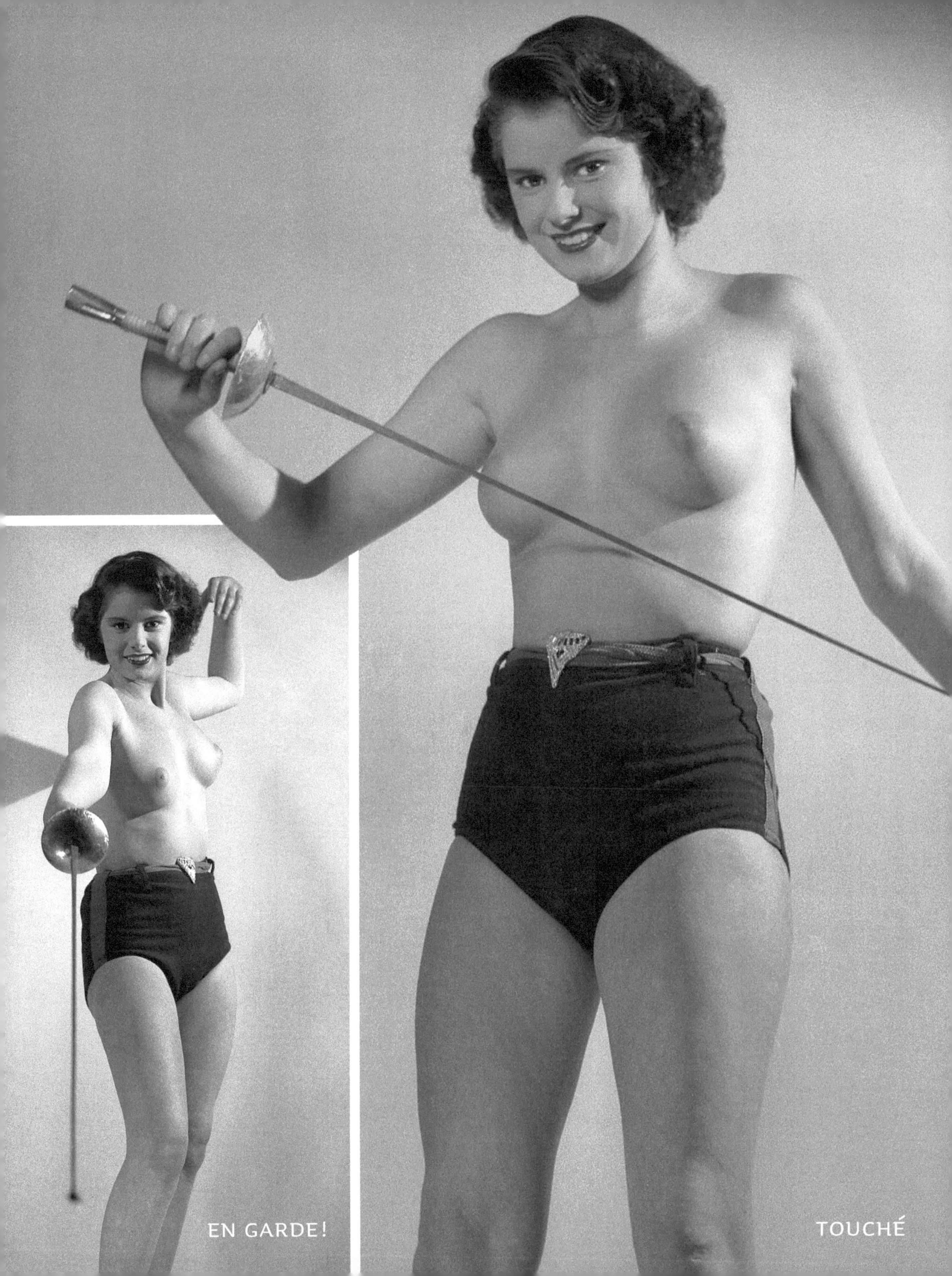
EN GARDE!
TOUCHÉ

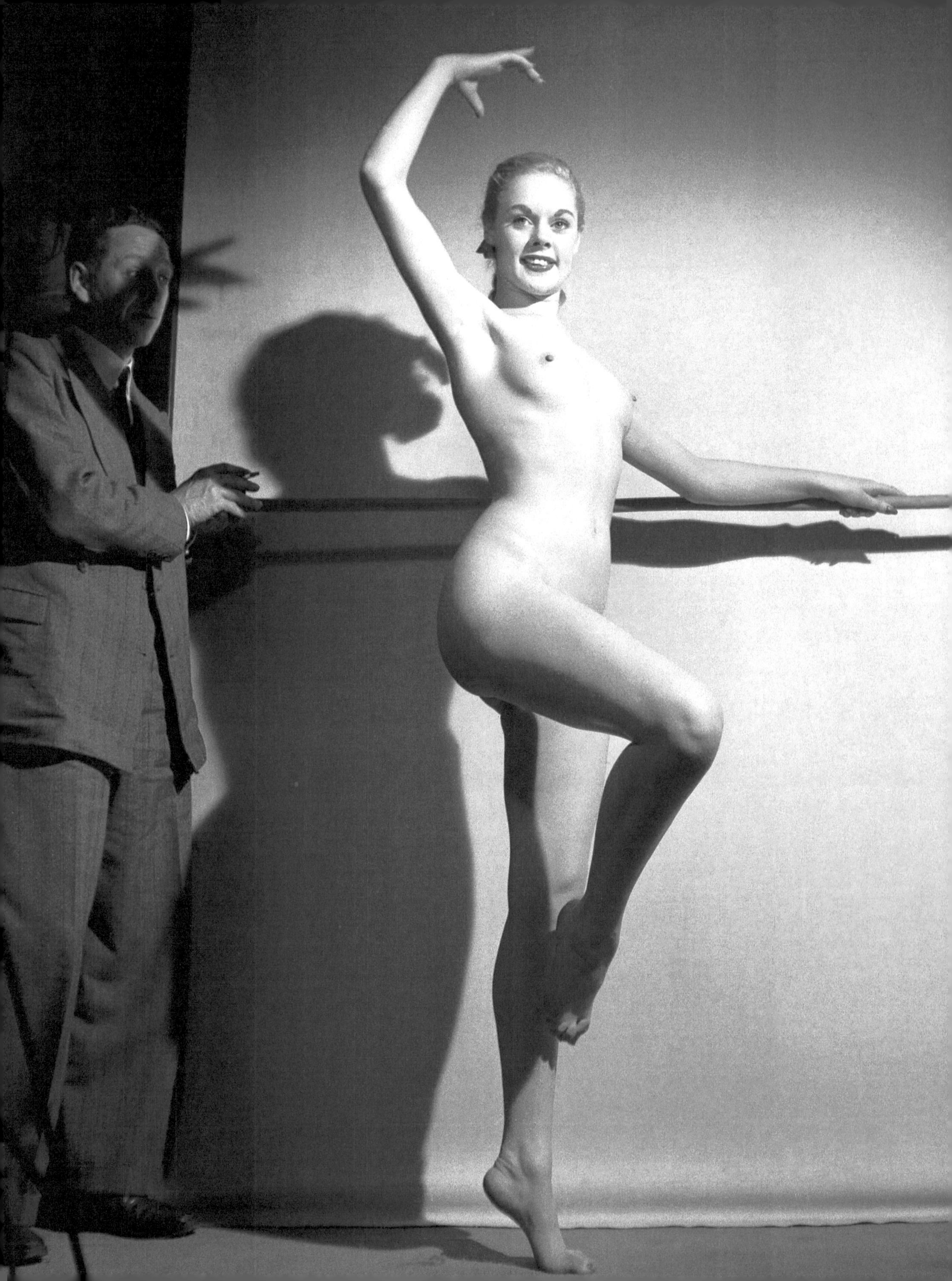

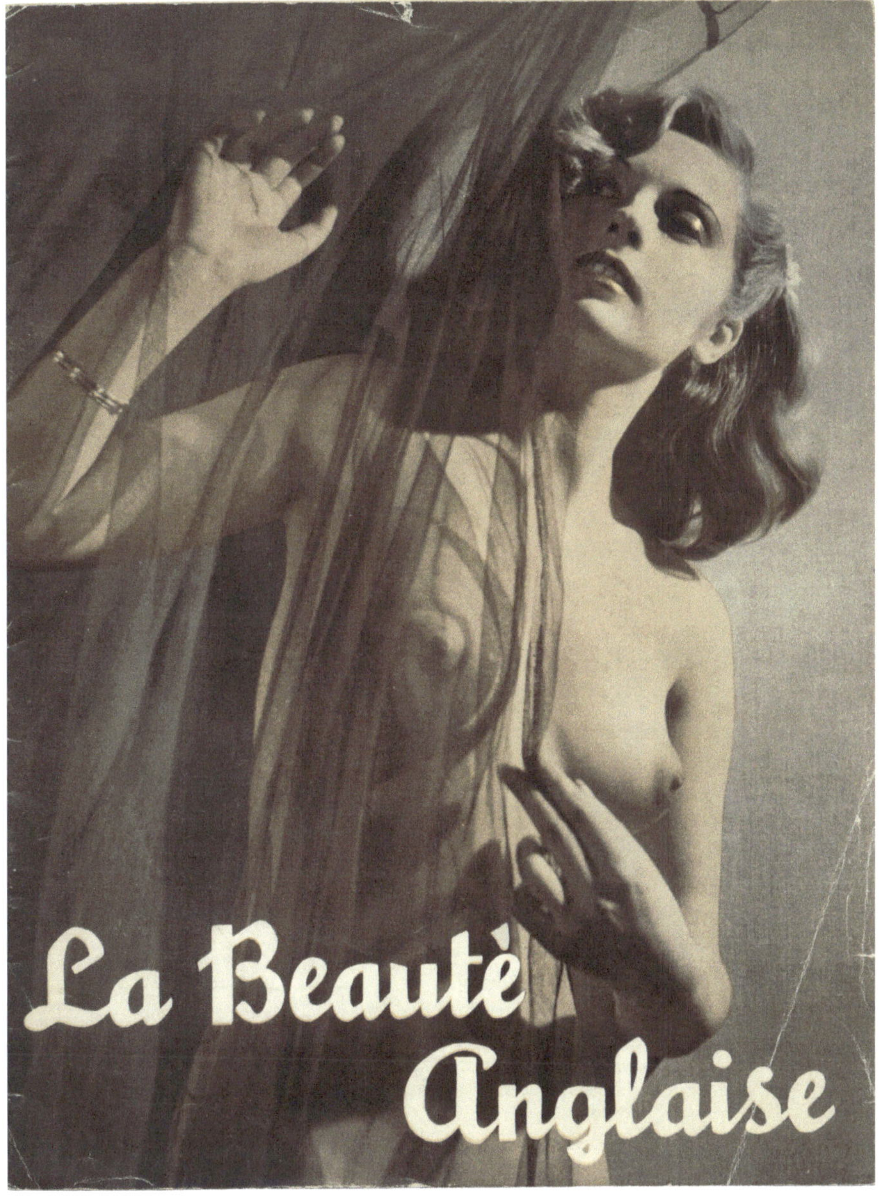

Left: *La Beauté Anglaise*, with photography by Stephen Glass, John Spencer & Co., Shepherds Bush, London, circa 1956. In this publication the publishers have, in their own words, "tried to give the Art world a series of studies which are typical of the beauty of the feminine charm of our isles. The student of Art will, it is hoped, appreciate the presentation."

Far left: An associate of Stephen Glass watches on as a model poses at the barre.

One of Zoltán's clients was Odhams Press, which published *Lilliput*, a celebrated pocket-sized gentleman's magazine that featured an assortment of titillating articles and risqué humour, together with adventurous photographic essays by such well-known talents as Bill Brandt and Brassai. As Zoltán's reputation grew, he was dubbed "Picasso with a camera".

Meanwhile, Stephen made a name for himself taking pictures for continental magazines such as *Paris Hollywood, Femina,* and *Modelstudier.* However, he is best remembered for the work he did for *The Naturist* and *Health and Efficiency.*

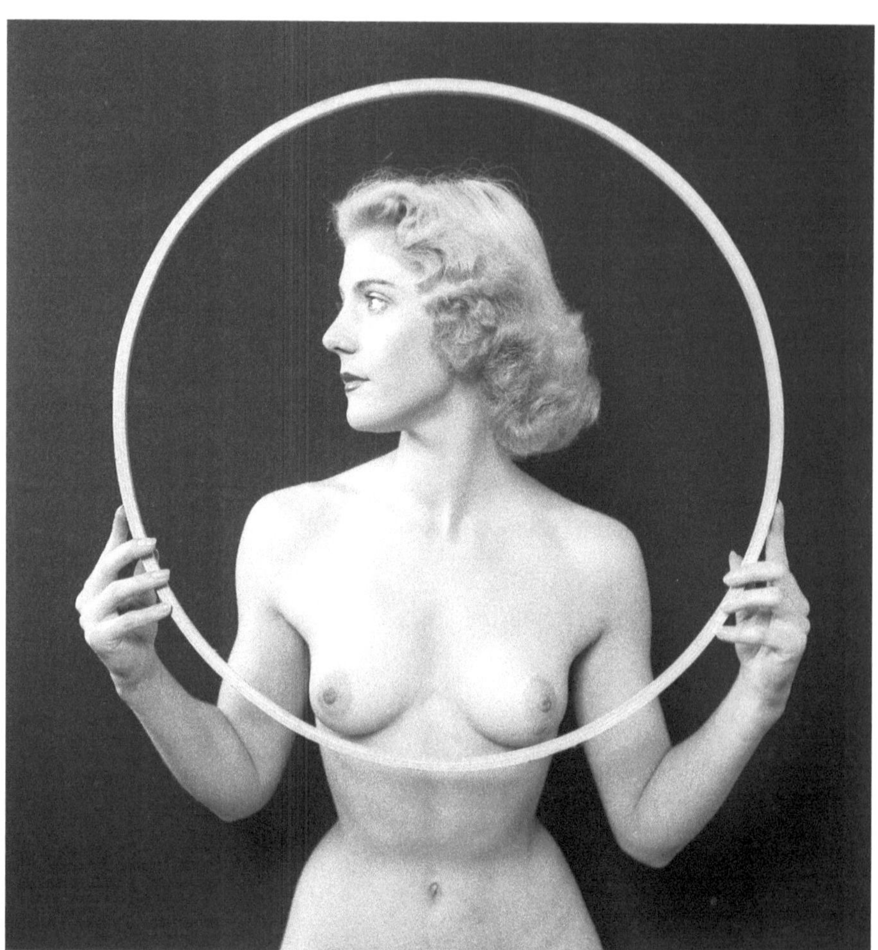

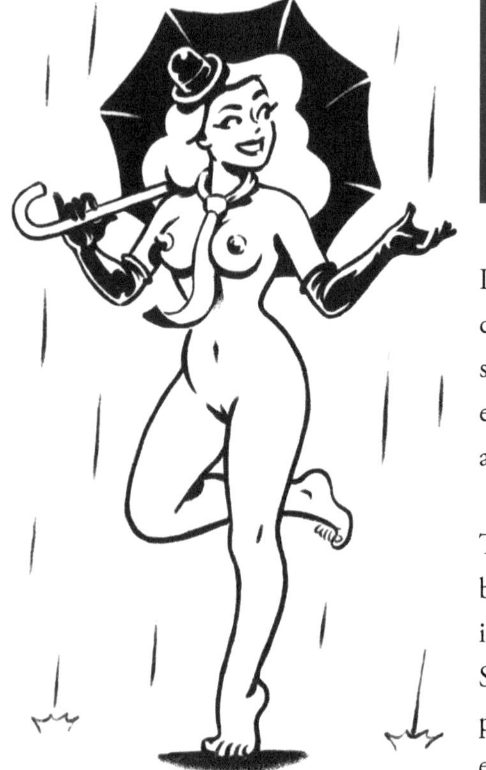

In a rare interview he gave to *Health and Efficiency* magazine in 1951, Stephen confessed he was extremely interested in the fine arts, as well as being a keen sports enthusiast. Readers were also told that he played the cello and was an expert on physical training; at the time, he never missed his daily PT exercises and attended weightlifting and bodybuilding classes every week.

The well-known model Pamela Green (1929–2010) posed for both Glass brothers on several occasions: for Stephen at the infamous nudist camp Spielplatz in Bricket Wood, Hertfordshire, and at his tiny first-floor studio in Old Church Street in London's Chelsea, just off the King's Road. "In those days when Stephen photographed me, I still had dark hair," Pamela recalled. "He liked his props, especially the stuffed animals." Pamela's agent, Pearl Beresford, sent her along to Zoltán Glass, whose studio on the King's Road was enormous by comparison. Unlike Stephen, Zoltán was brisk and businesslike.

Iseult, the daughter of Spielplatz co-founders Charles and Dorothy Macaskie, remembers Stephen. "He would often ask me to pose for him," she said. "I quite enjoyed having my photo taken, but when I asked to be paid, he stopped using me. A bit of pocket money back then would have been nice."

As well as magazines, Stephen Glass's work graced a series of small books published by The Naturist Ltd., including *Sussex Maidens* (1949), *The Pool of Enchantment* (1950), and *Nudist Life in Spielplatz* (1956). He also photographed the popular model June Palmer (1940–2004). The photos in this book are from his uncensored negatives. Until the end of the 1960s, it was considered obscene to show pubic hair or genitalia in British publications. To ensure that an image of a naked young lady would not incur the wrath of the censor, the model would shave down below, and the photograph would then be retouched by hand to erase anything problematic.

By 1964, Zoltán Glass had made enough money to sell his Chelsea studios to a consortium of British photographers. He then moved to a villa in Roquebrune on the French Riviera with his common-law wife Pat, a former cabaret dancer. He offered his collection of pin-up photography to glamour photographer Harrison Marks who, strangely, turned it down. Zoltán died in France on February 24, 1981, at the age of 78, leaving neither offspring nor a will. His photographs were eventually given to The National Science and Media Museum in Bradford, Yorkshire. Stephen Glass died on April 23, 1990. His work ended up at auction.

Left: Magazine advert for the book *The Pool of Enchantment*, published by The Naturist Ltd. in 1950.

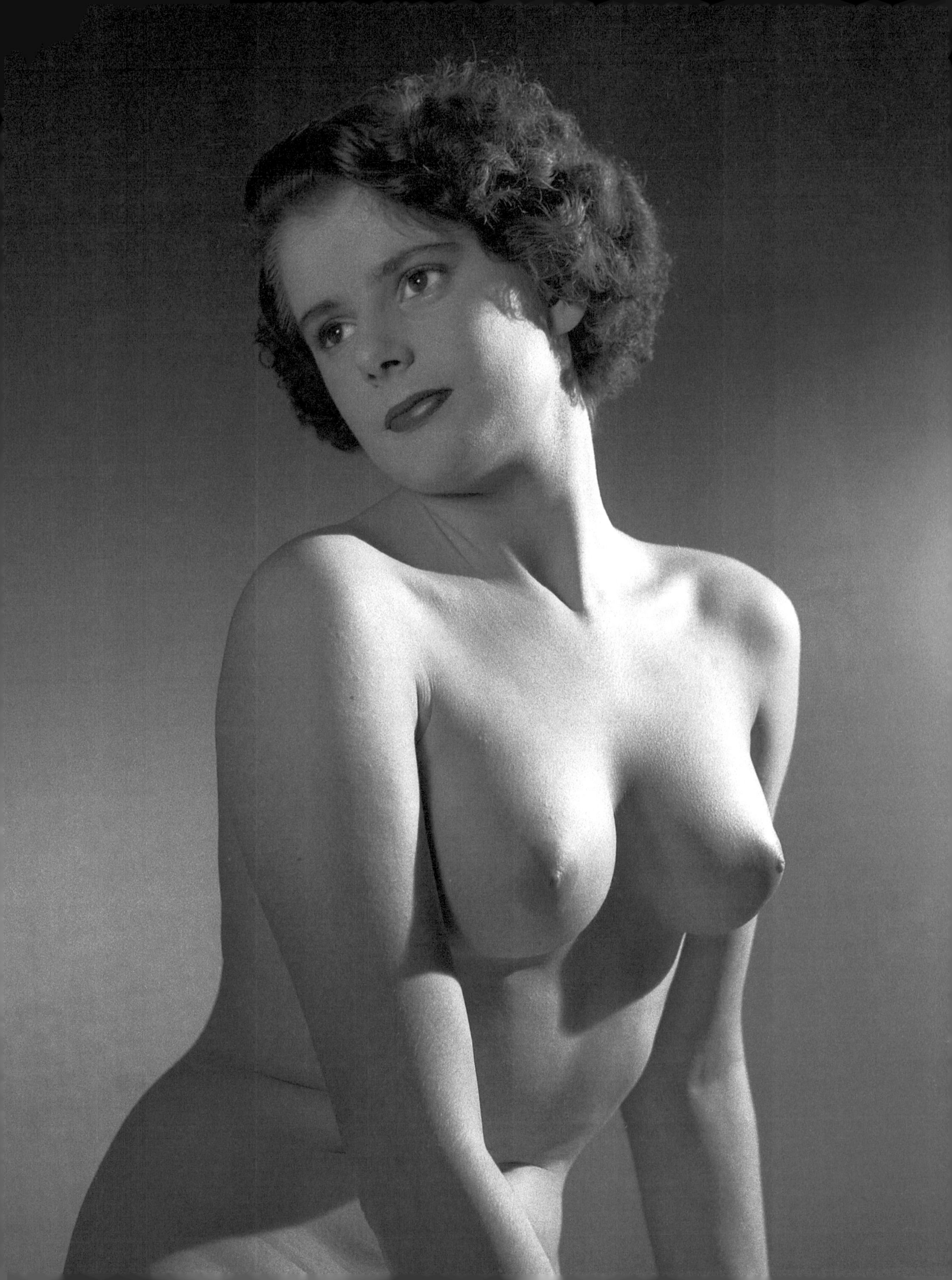

Pose & Poise is the seventh, and possibly the final (never say never), volume in Wolfbait's Stephen Glass Collection. The graceful studies featured here will no doubt help cement Glass's reputation as one of the preeminent, if not the most prolific, photographers of the female nude in the post-war period.

Glass's studio photographs celebrate the beauty of the female form in a great variety of moods and artistic senses. Every artist has their tricks of the trade and Stephen Glass was no exception. He made skilful use of light and shadow, but a key aspect of his work was his choice of model — the ladies' main criterion for selection was not being pretty, but being interesting. In this collection, the sure touch of the expert is revealed — the purposeful camera-artist who is not satisfied until he has reached something close to the ever-evasive notion of perfection.

The nude in art is a deep part of our psyche, culture, history, and iconography. The photographs featured in this volume disseminate so much healthy enjoyment of life that even the dim winter fog of London must give way. The young ladies may look French, but their appeal is universal, and nobody will question that they are pleasingly photogenic. For art lovers and connoisseurs such as yourself, this book is a simple, delightful pleasure.

Something about the female nude brings out the philosopher in me.

— B. Fotherington-Tomas

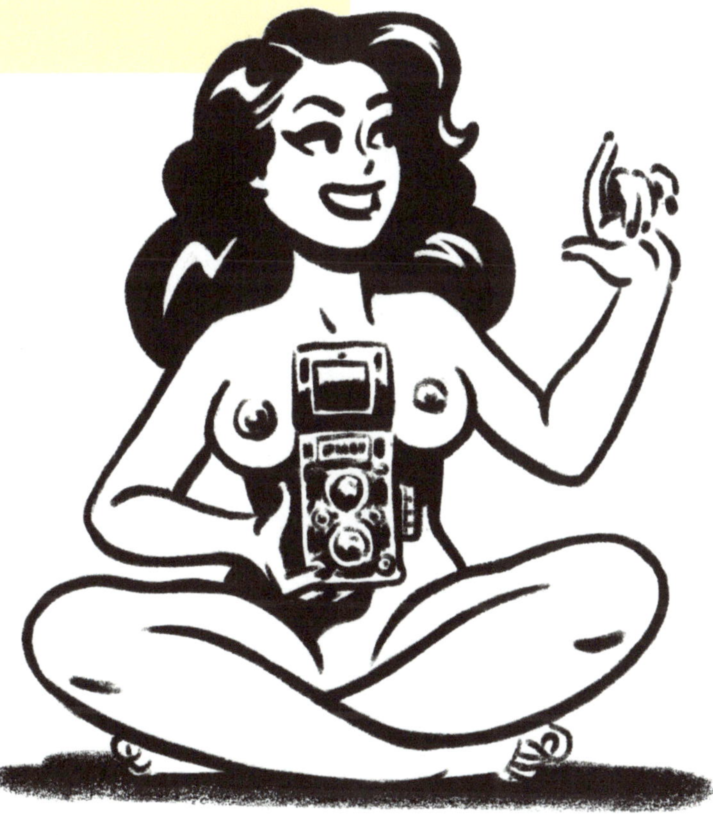

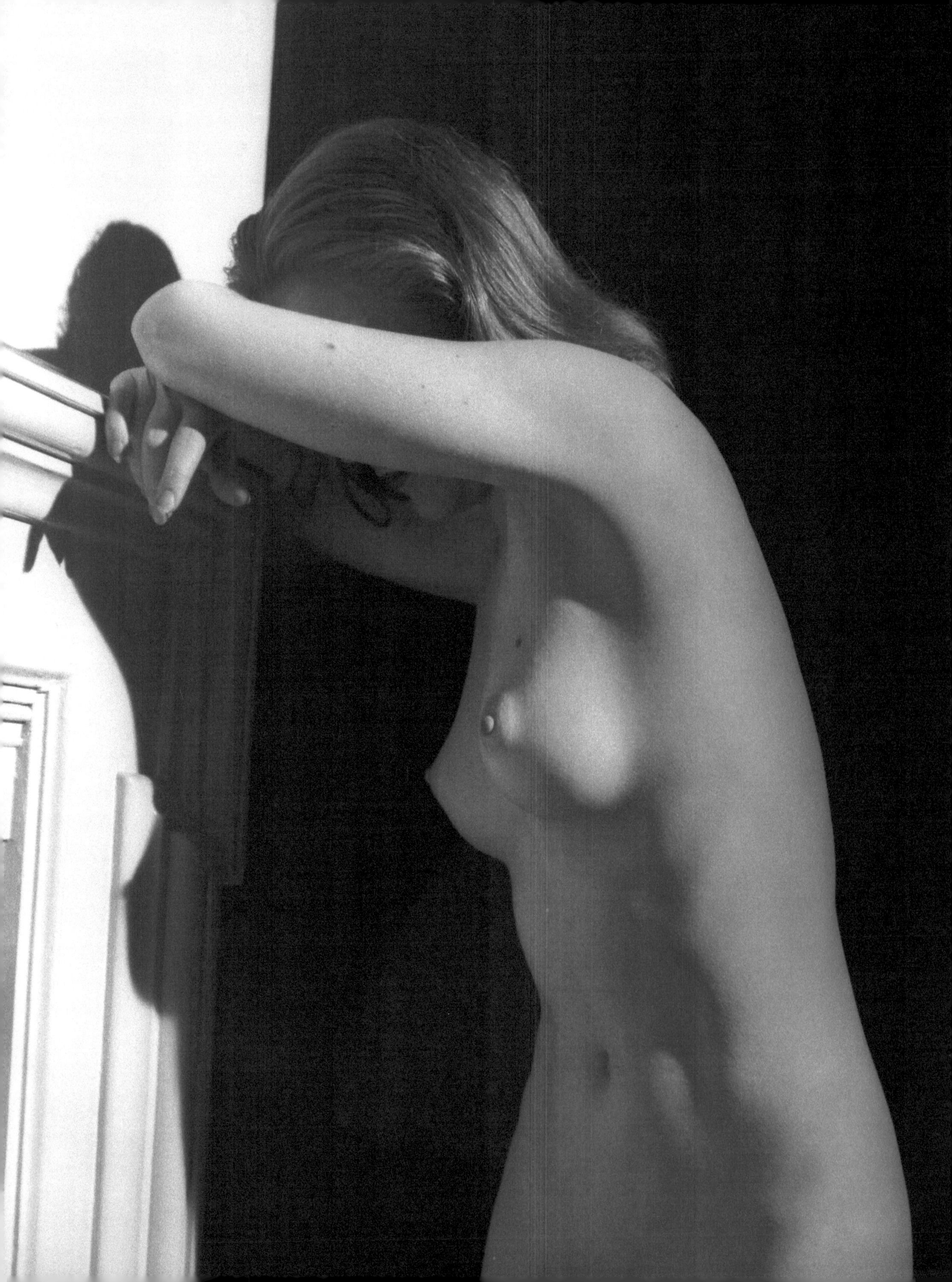

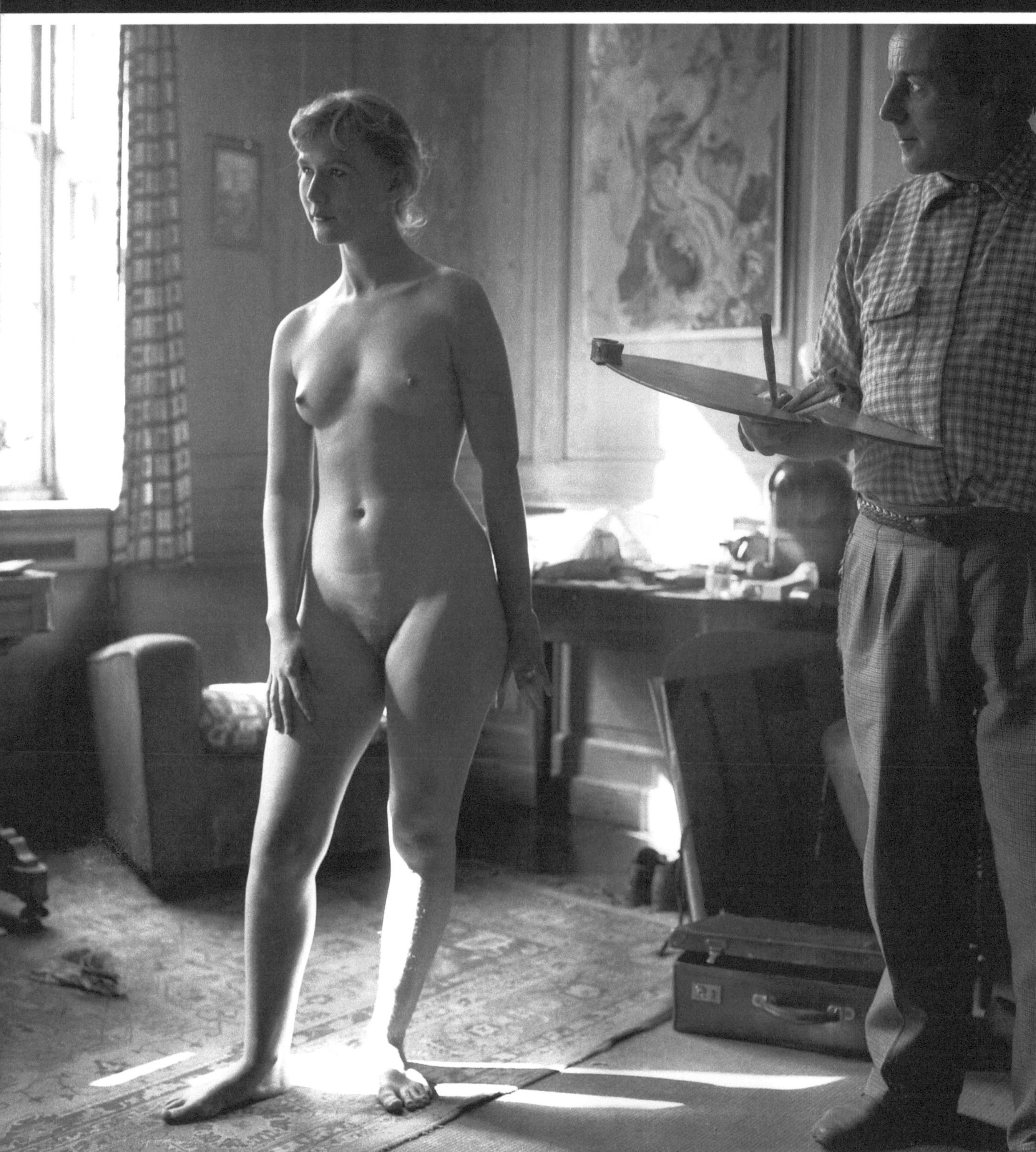

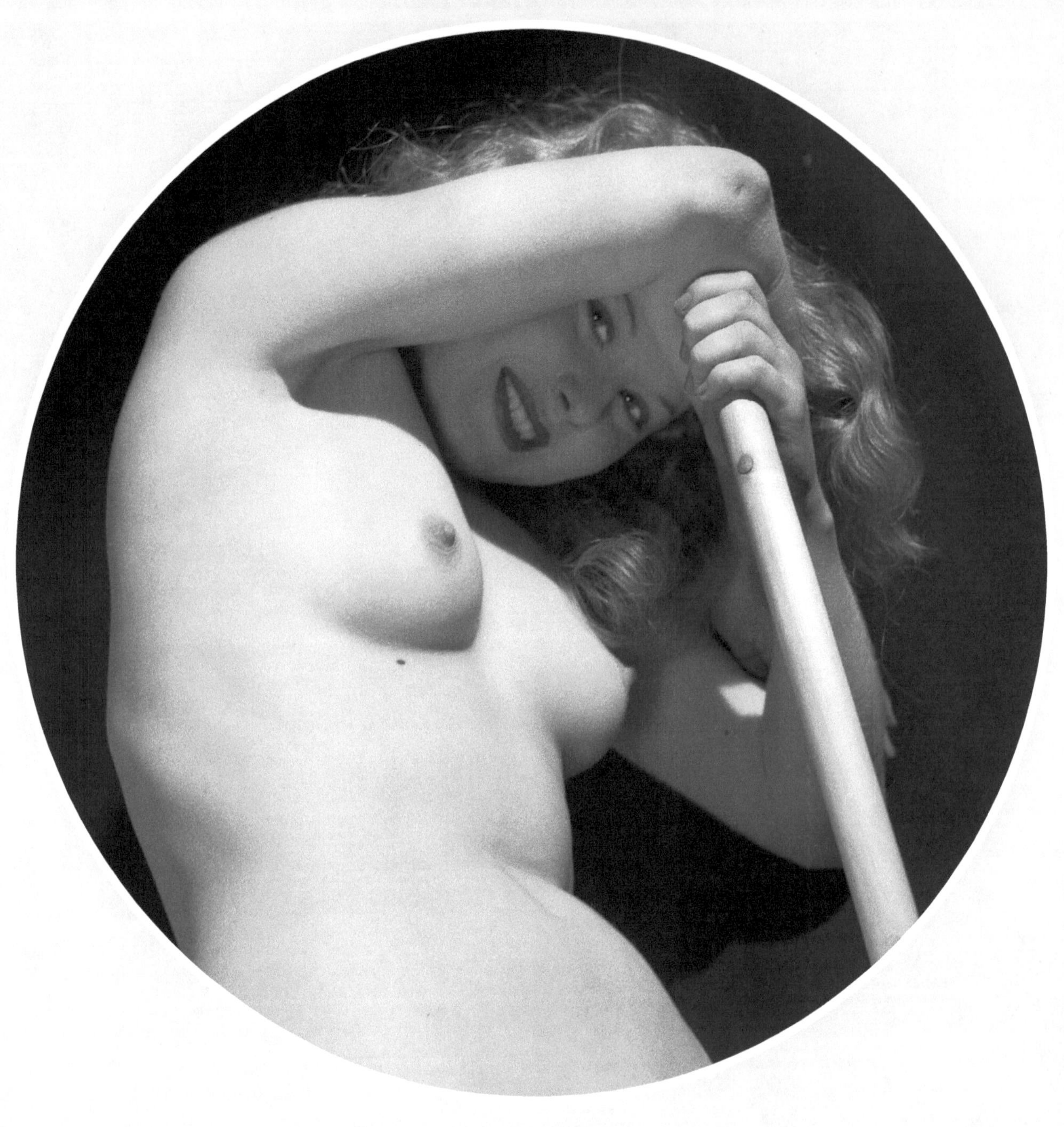

Above: Claudia Gray.

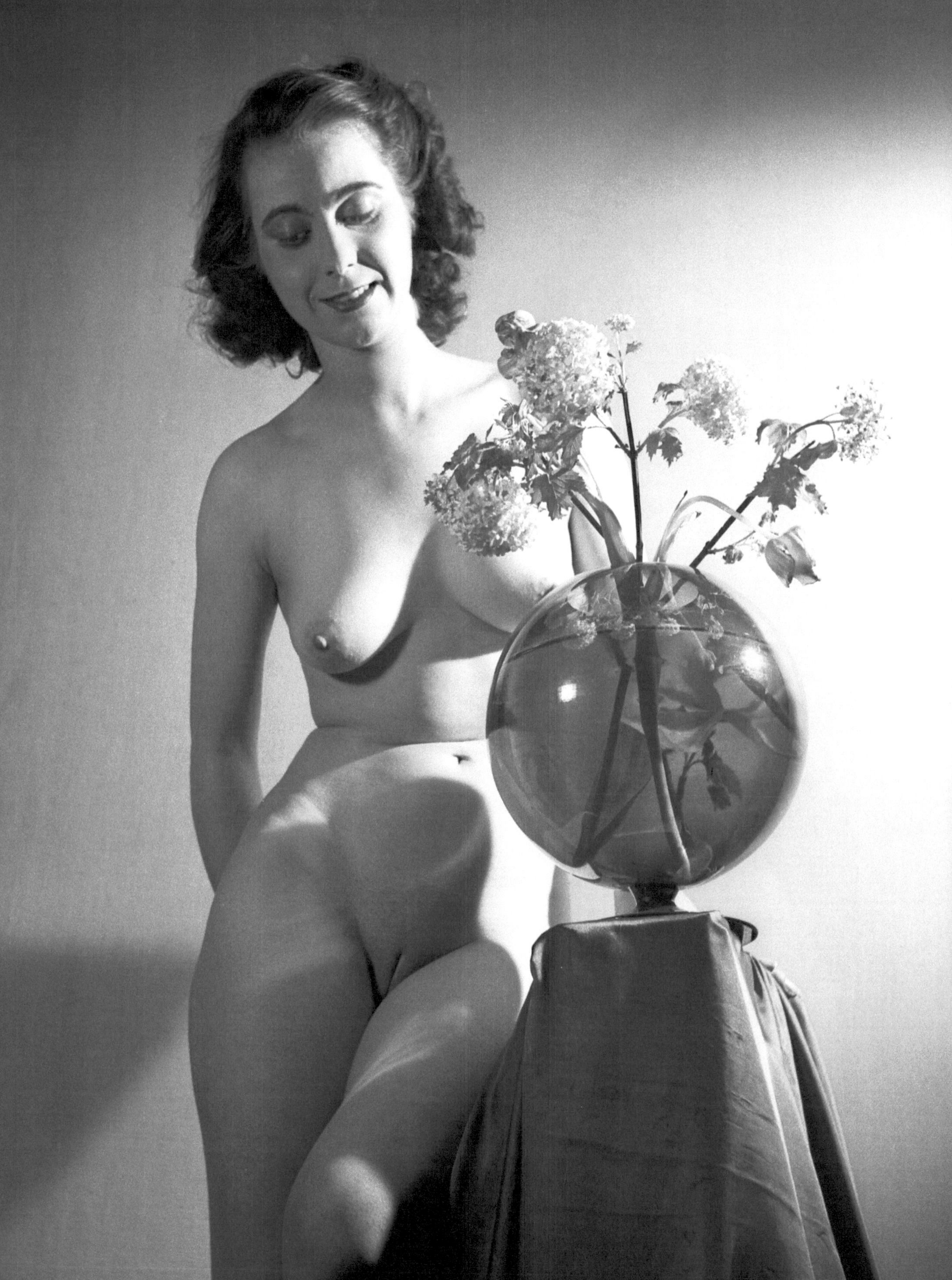

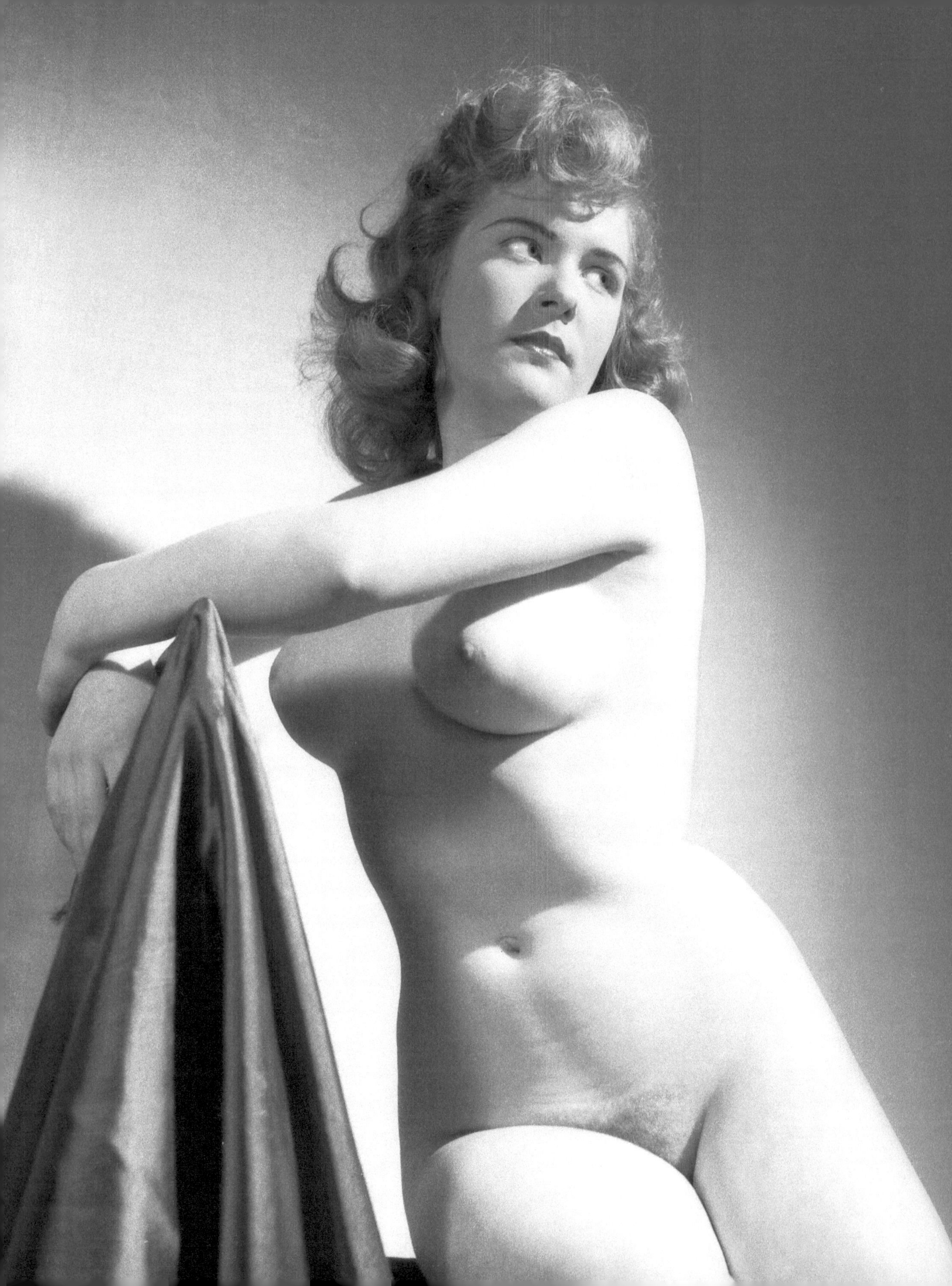

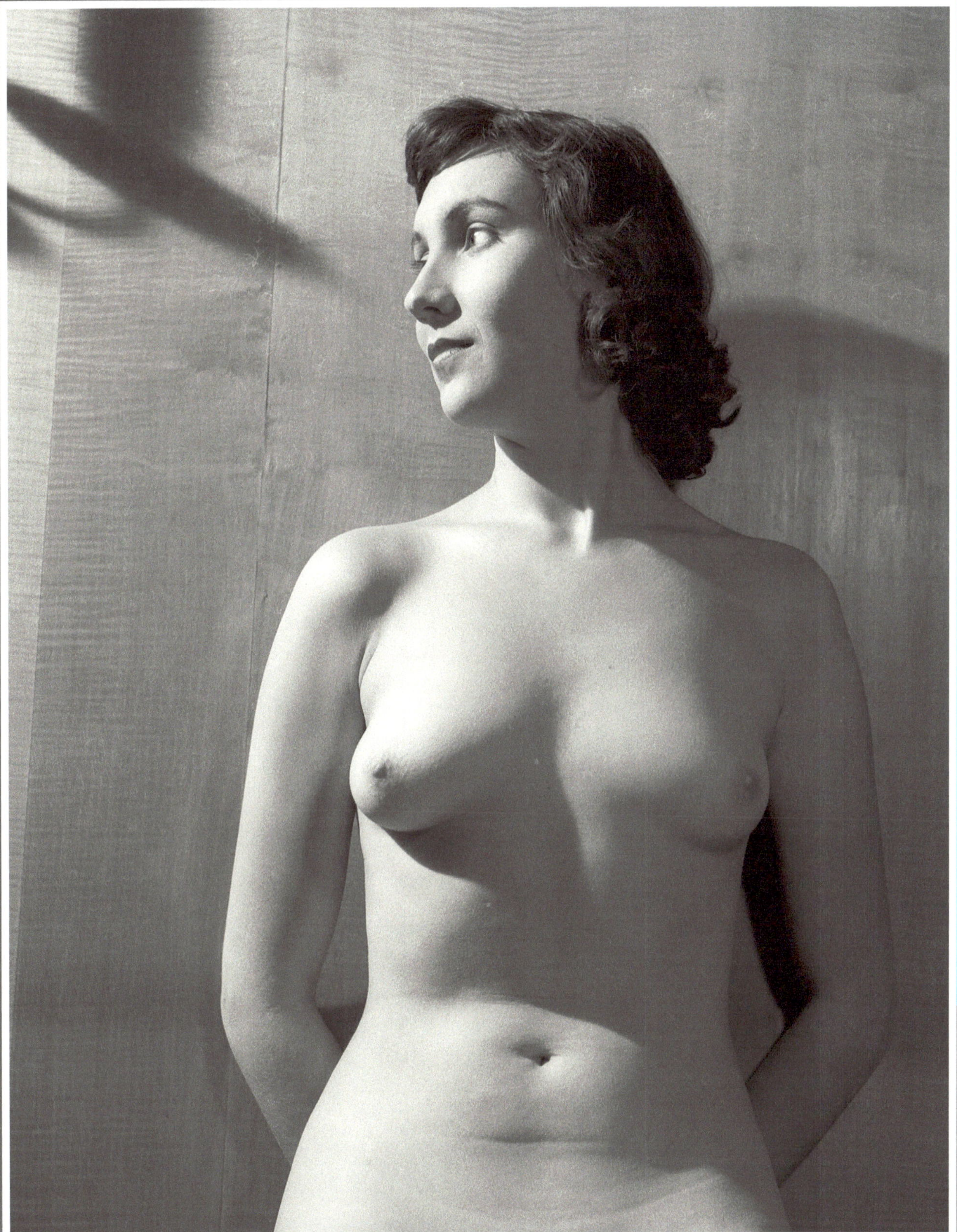

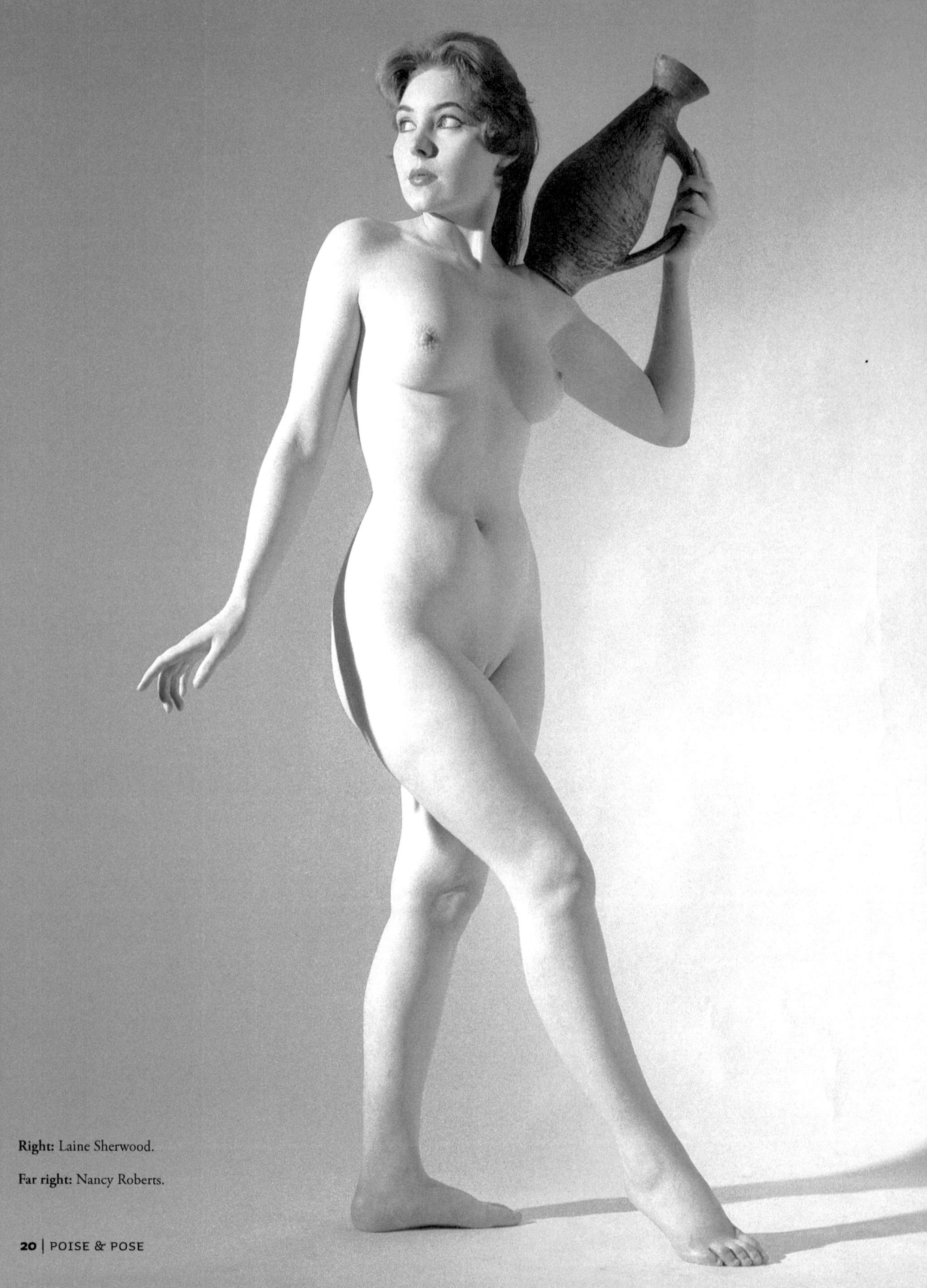

Right: Laine Sherwood.

Far right: Nancy Roberts.

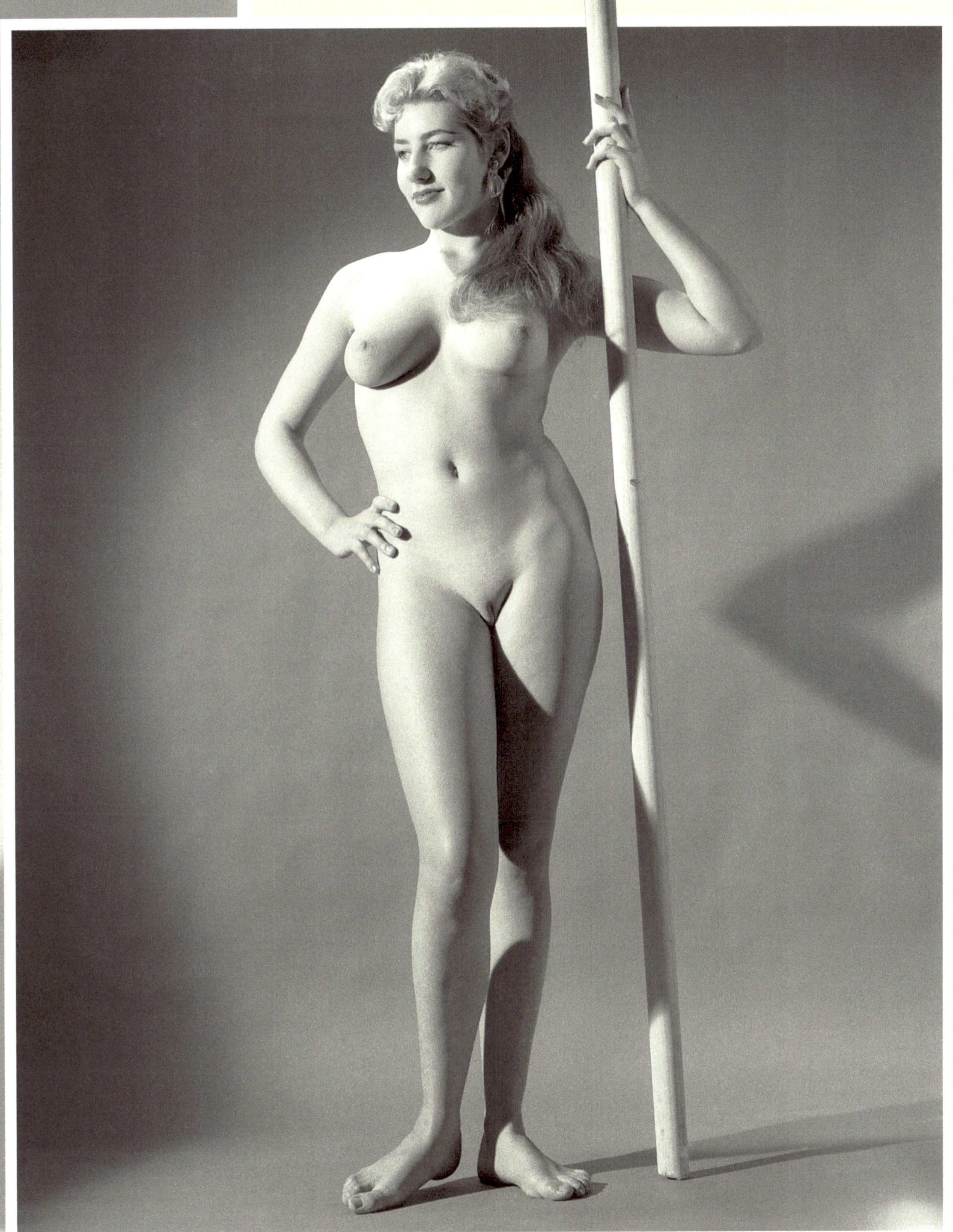

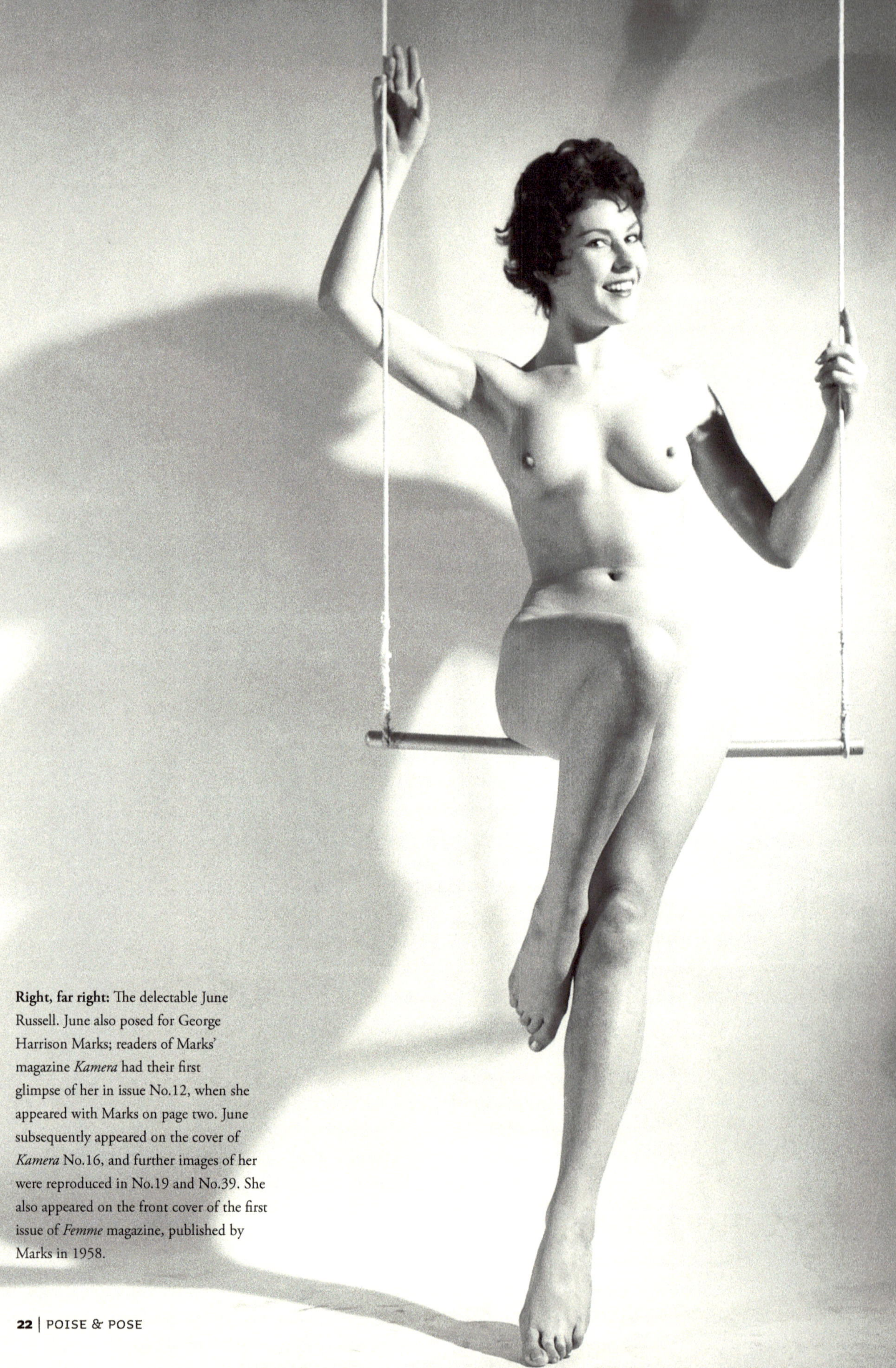

Right, far right: The delectable June Russell. June also posed for George Harrison Marks; readers of Marks' magazine *Kamera* had their first glimpse of her in issue No.12, when she appeared with Marks on page two. June subsequently appeared on the cover of *Kamera* No.16, and further images of her were reproduced in No.19 and No.39. She also appeared on the front cover of the first issue of *Femme* magazine, published by Marks in 1958.

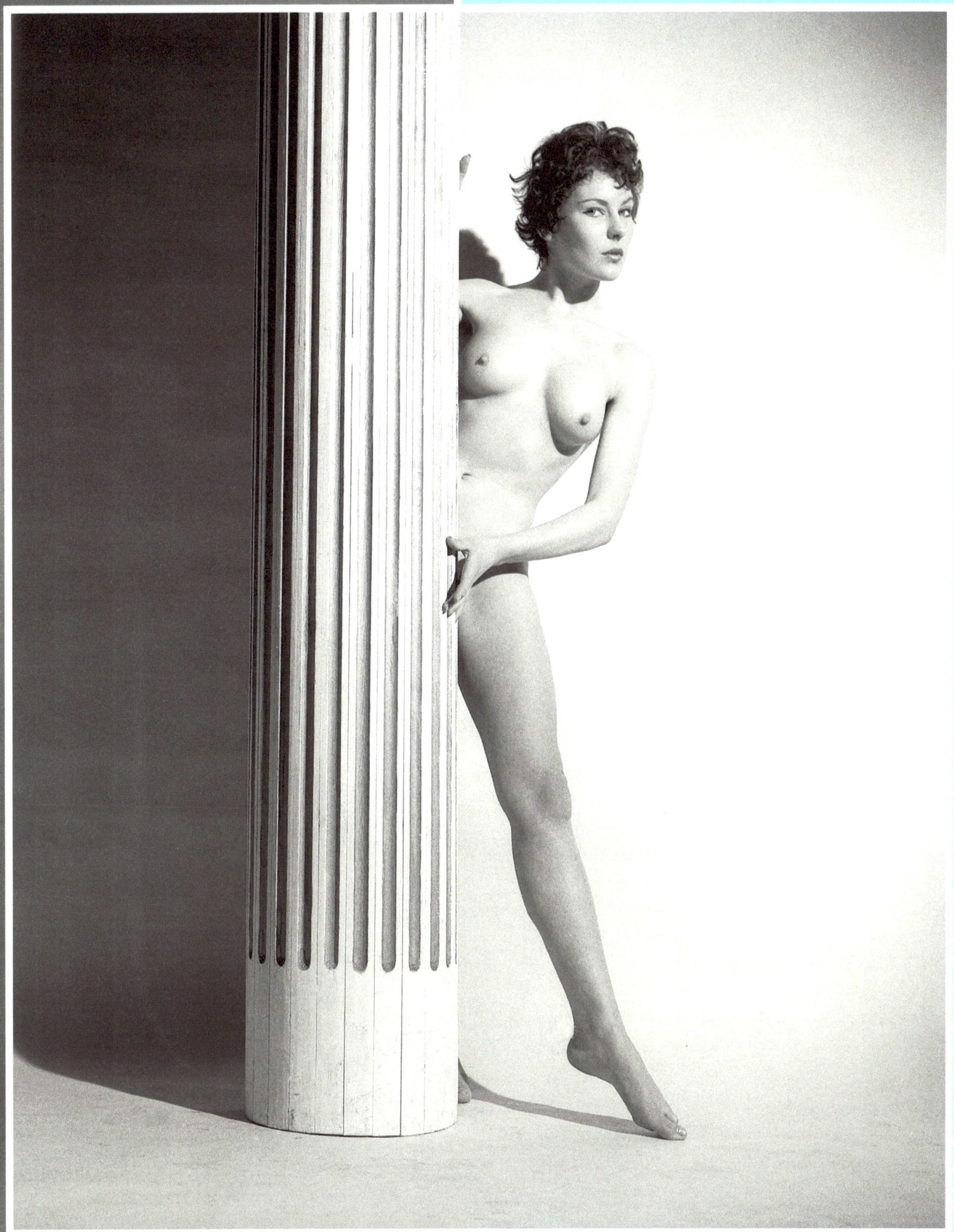

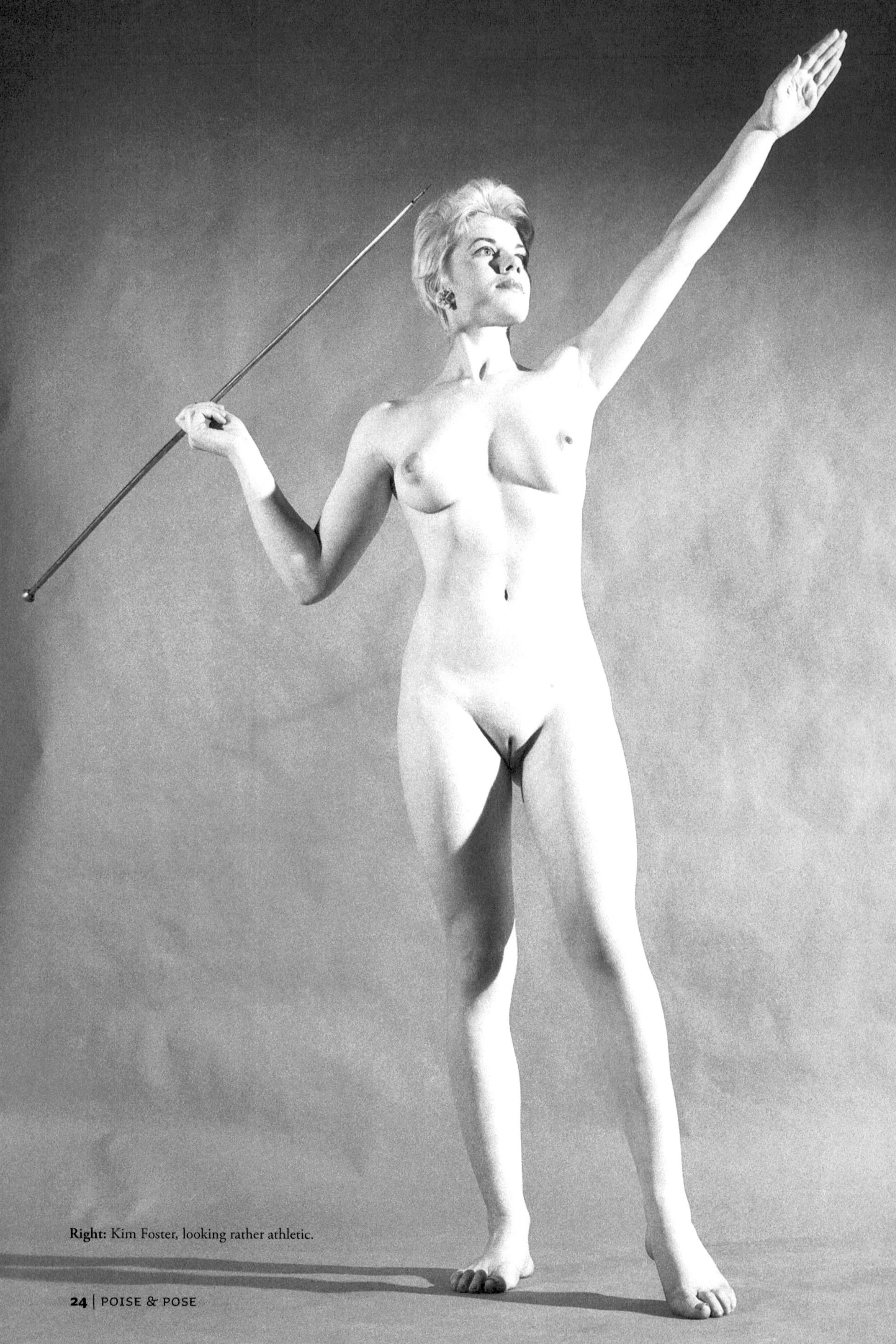

Right: Kim Foster, looking rather athletic.

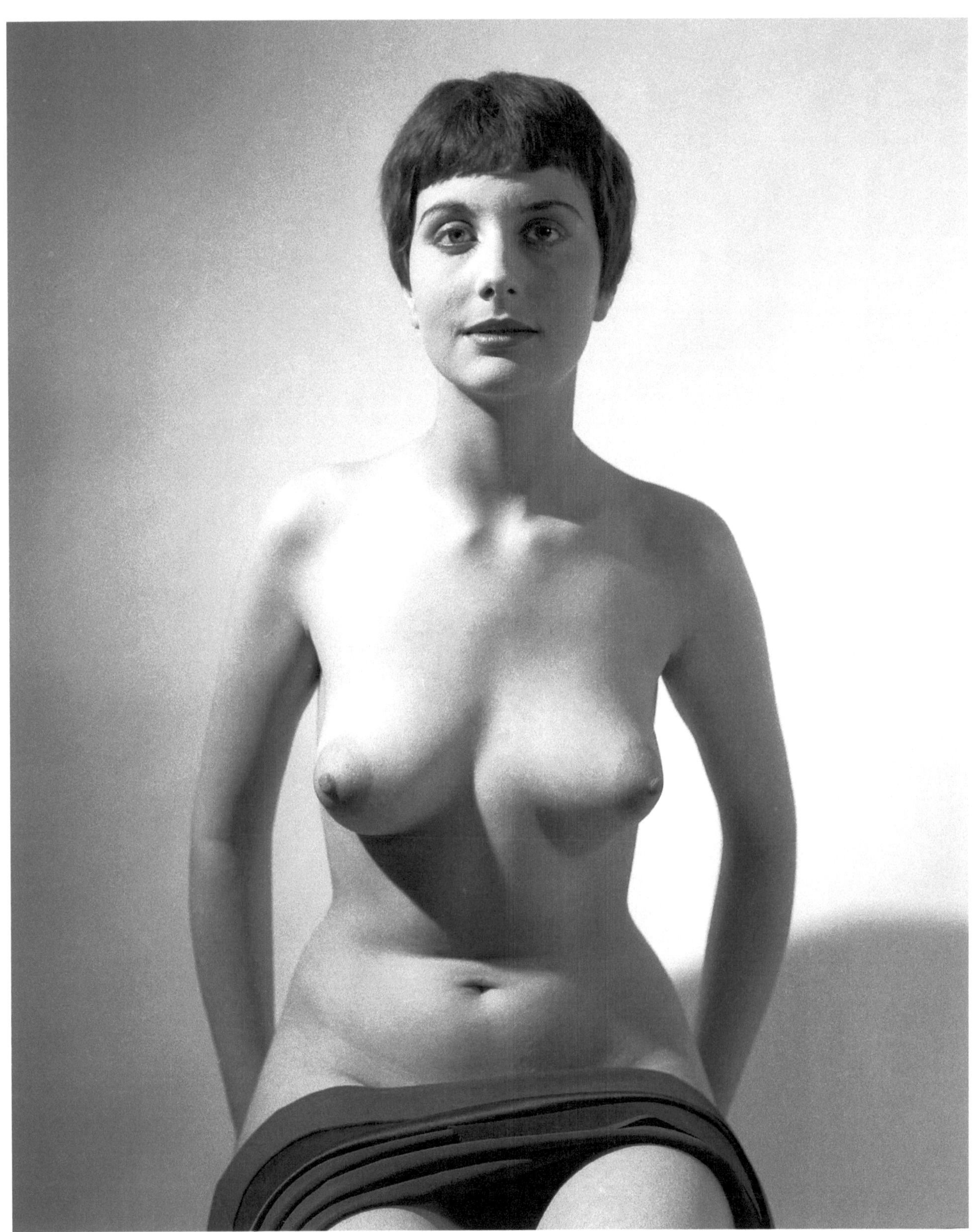

Above: The elegant Susan Rothwell.

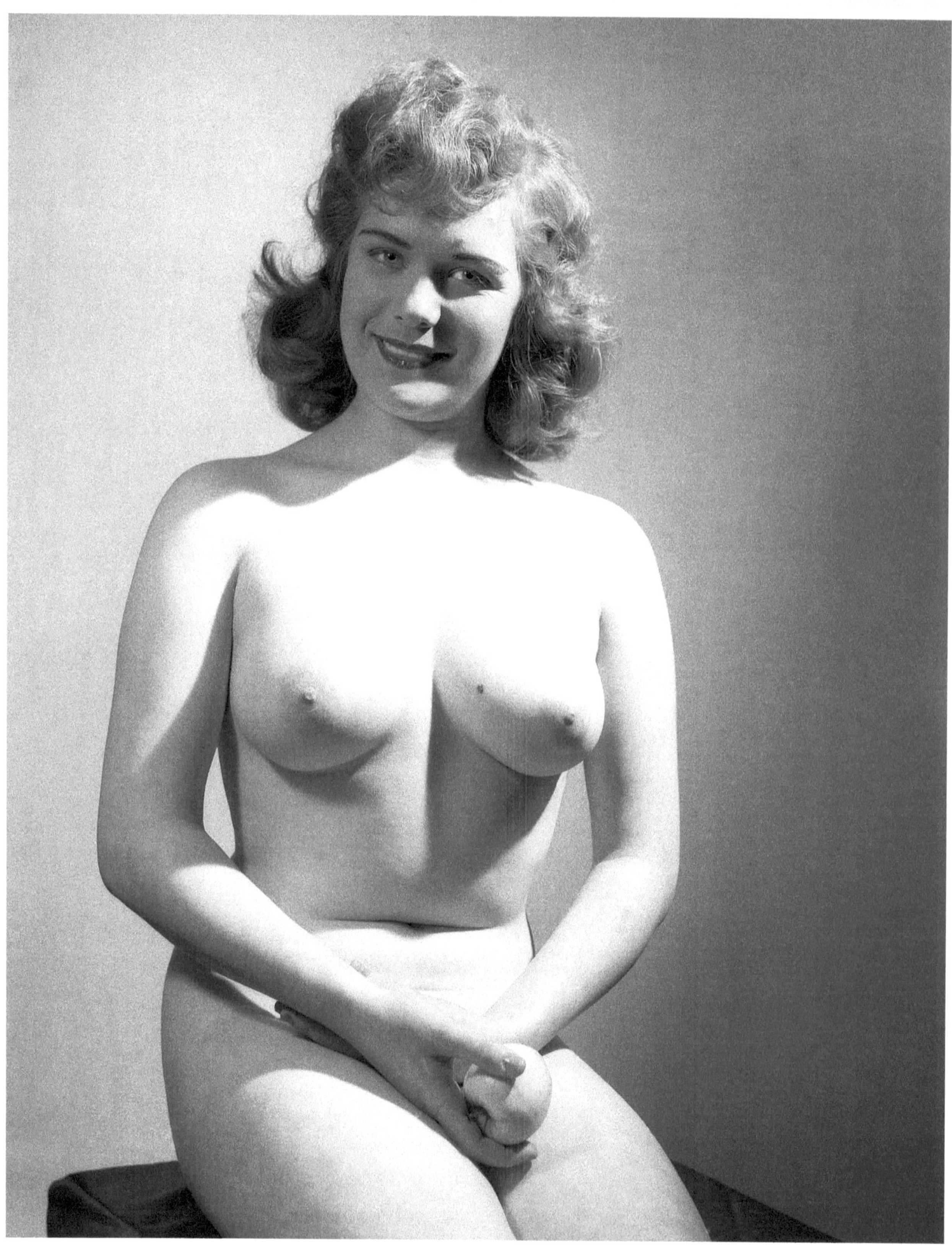

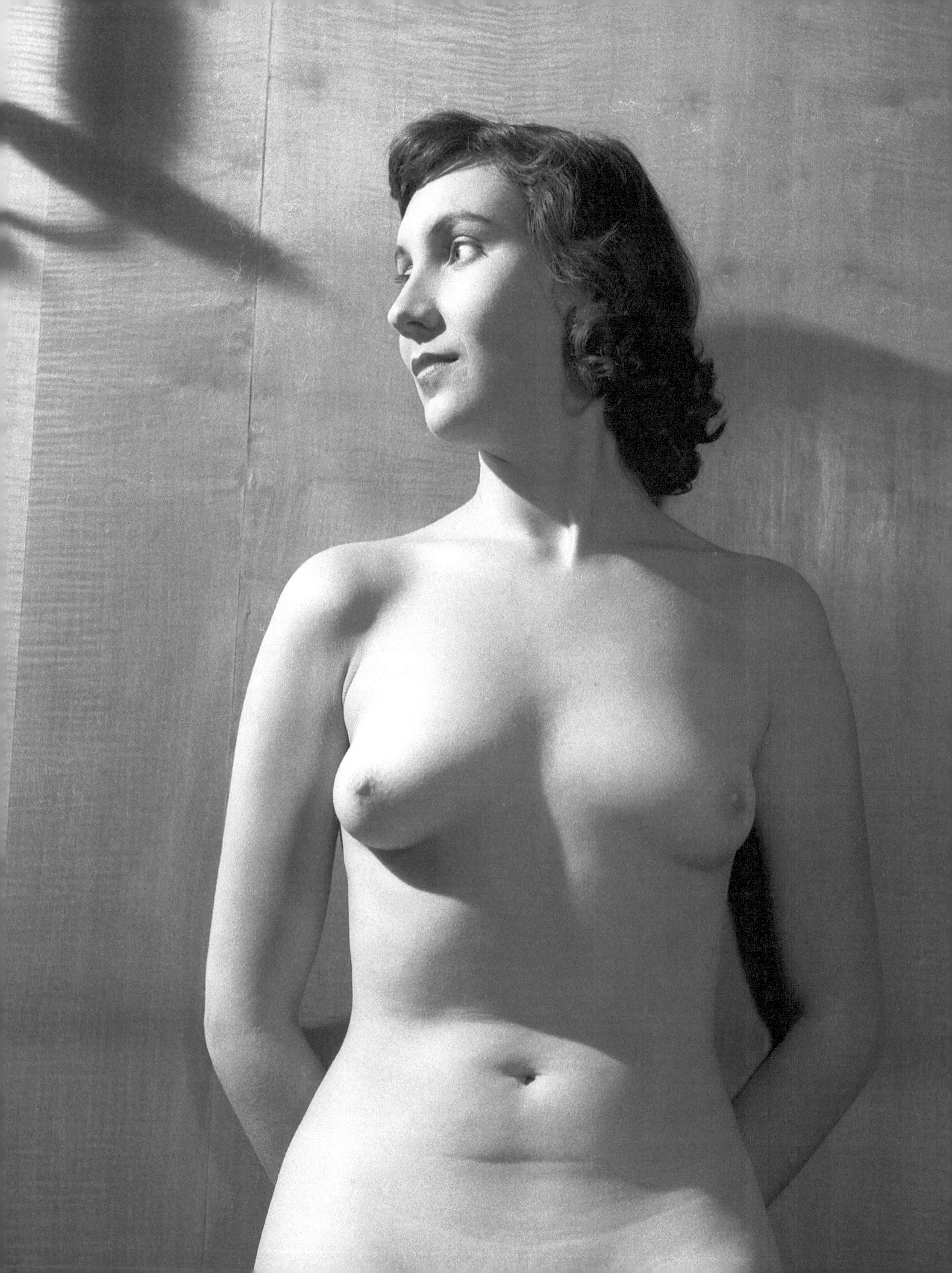

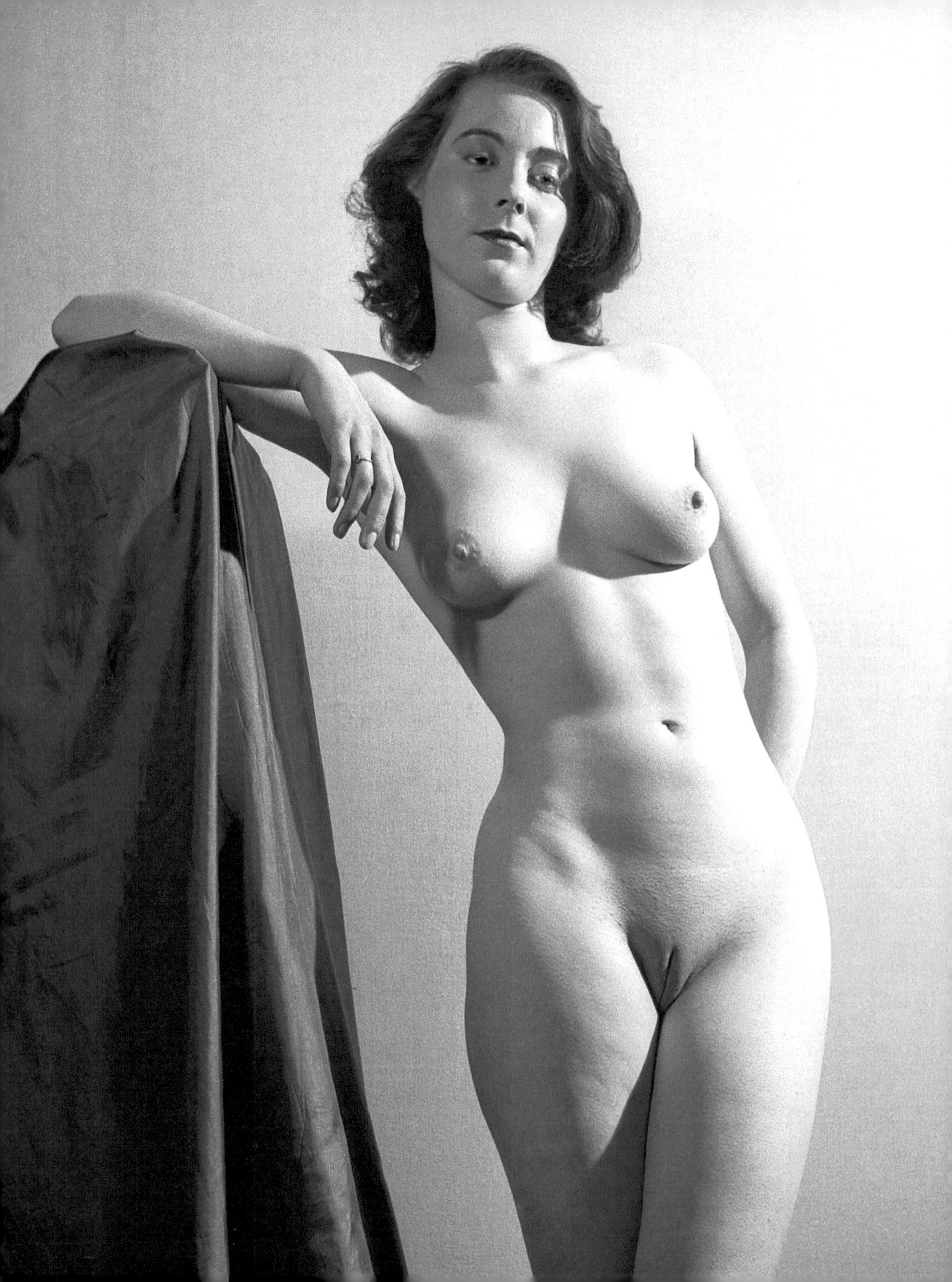

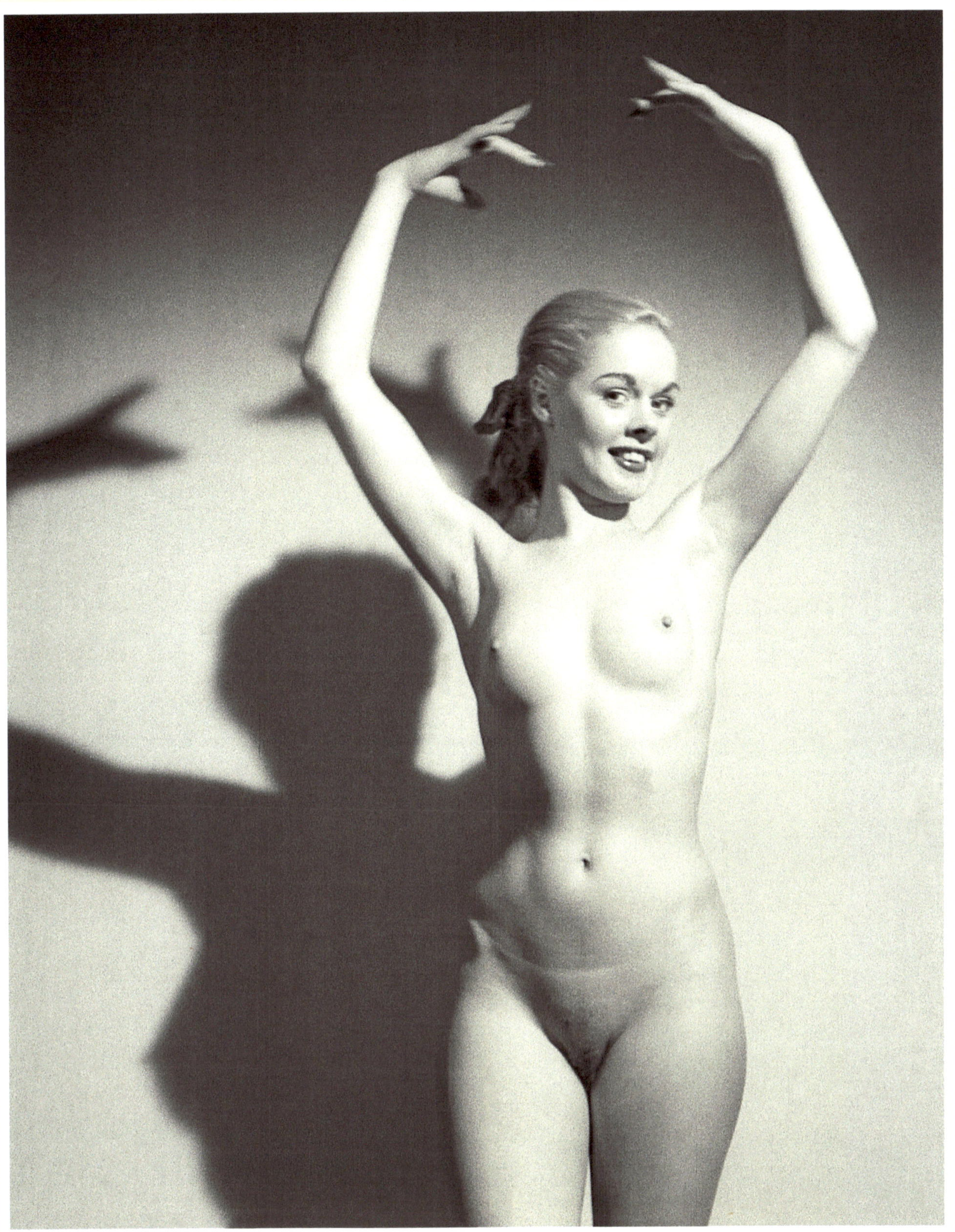

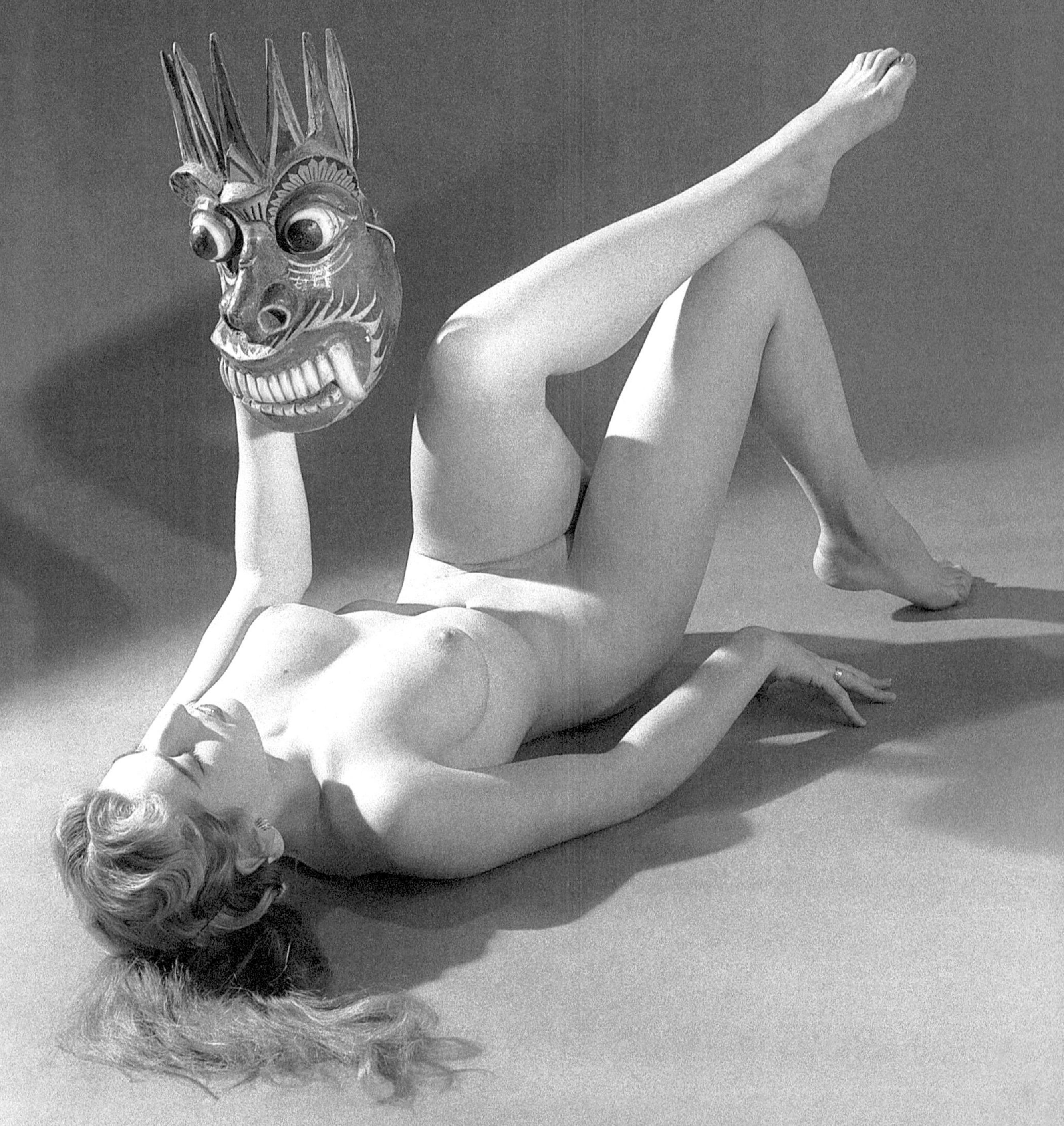

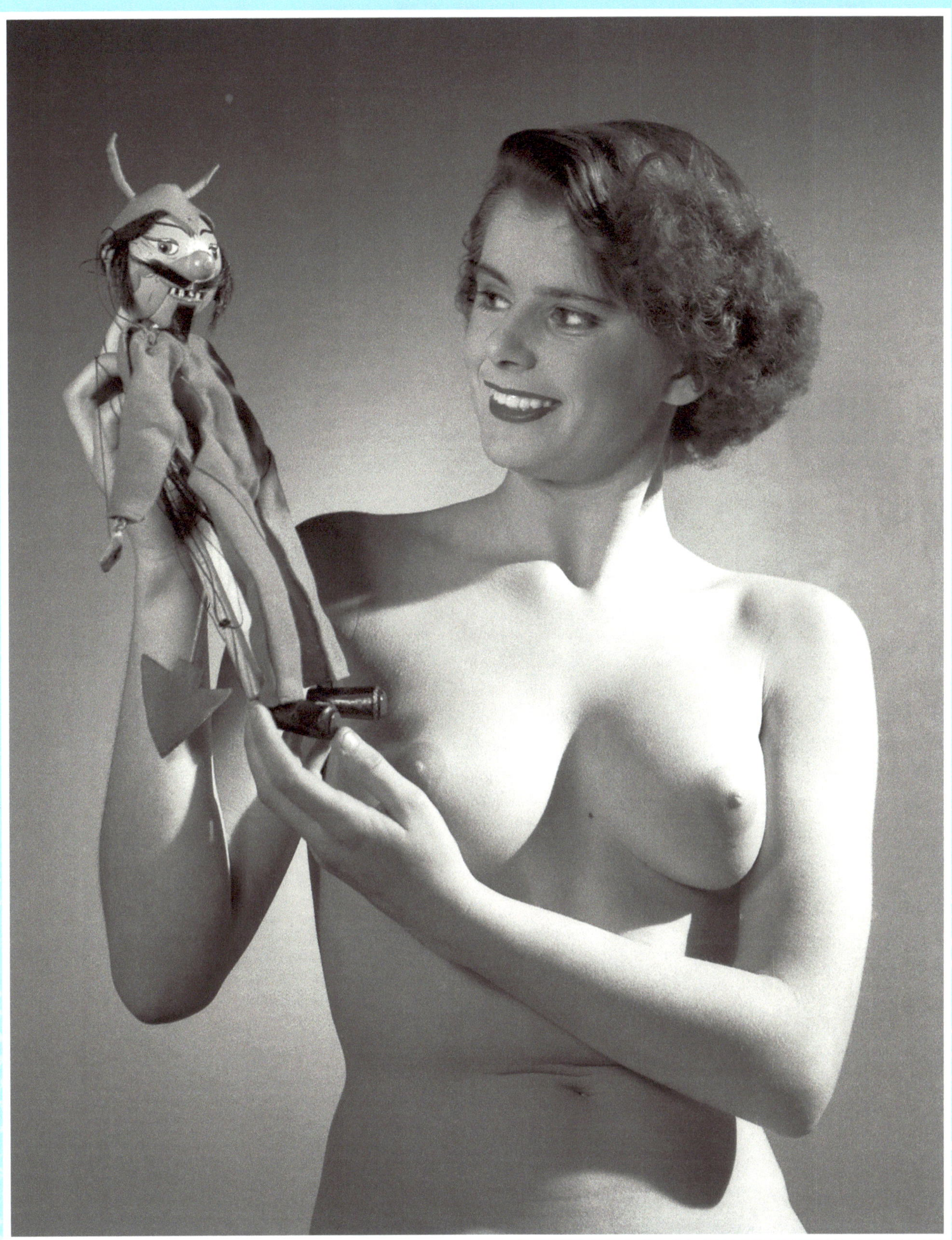

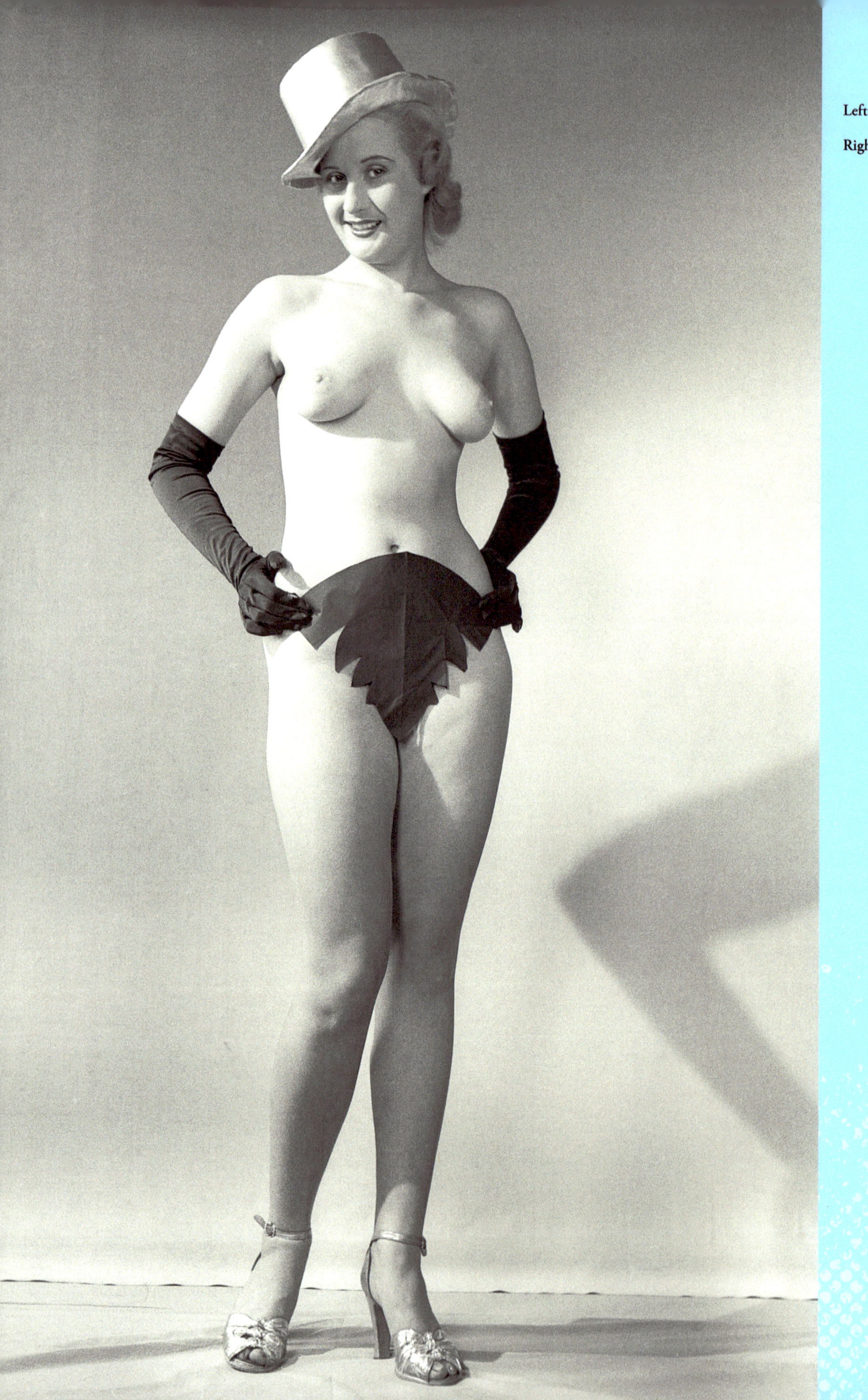

Left: Heather Biraks.

Right: Audrey Hill.

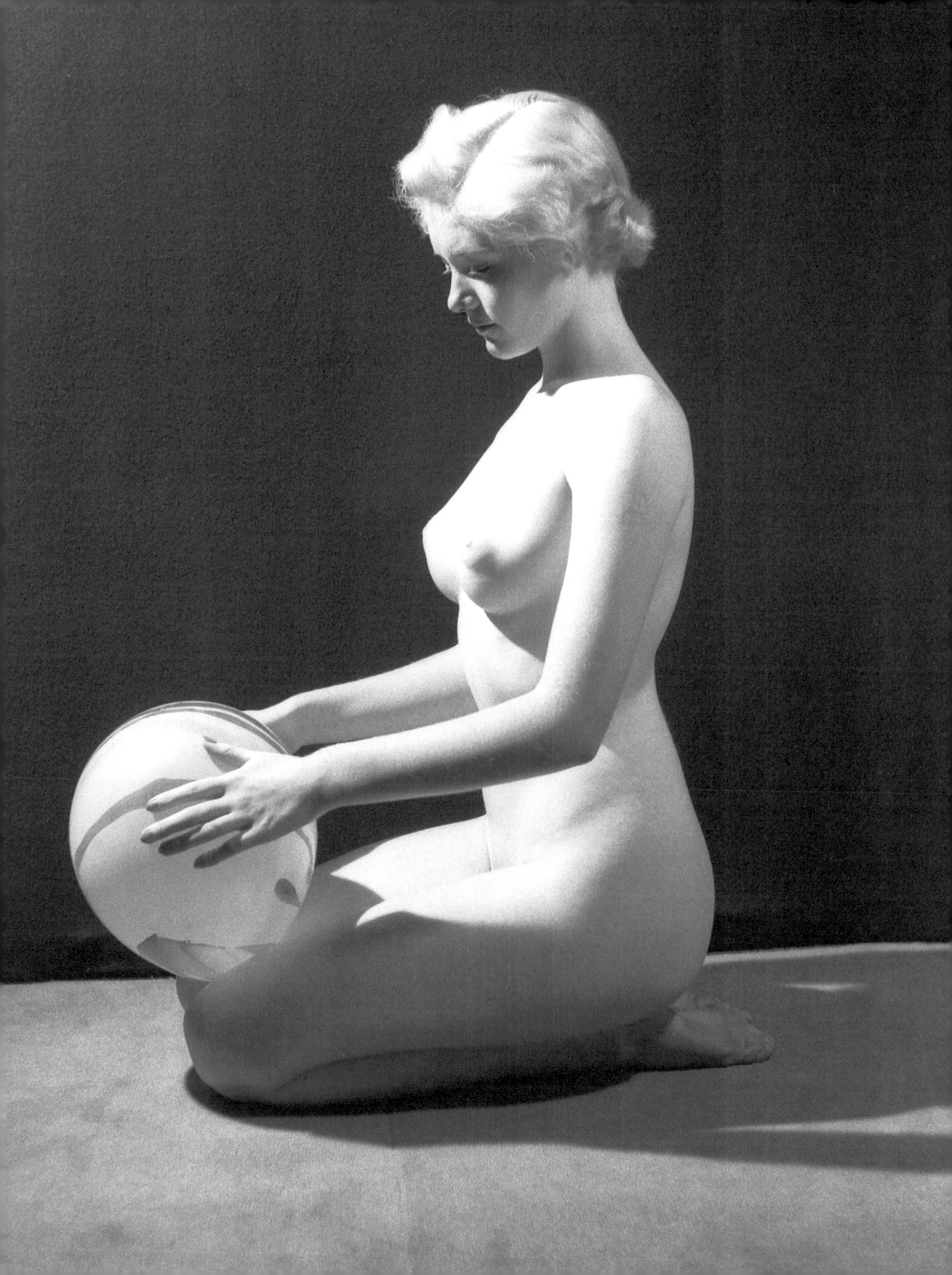

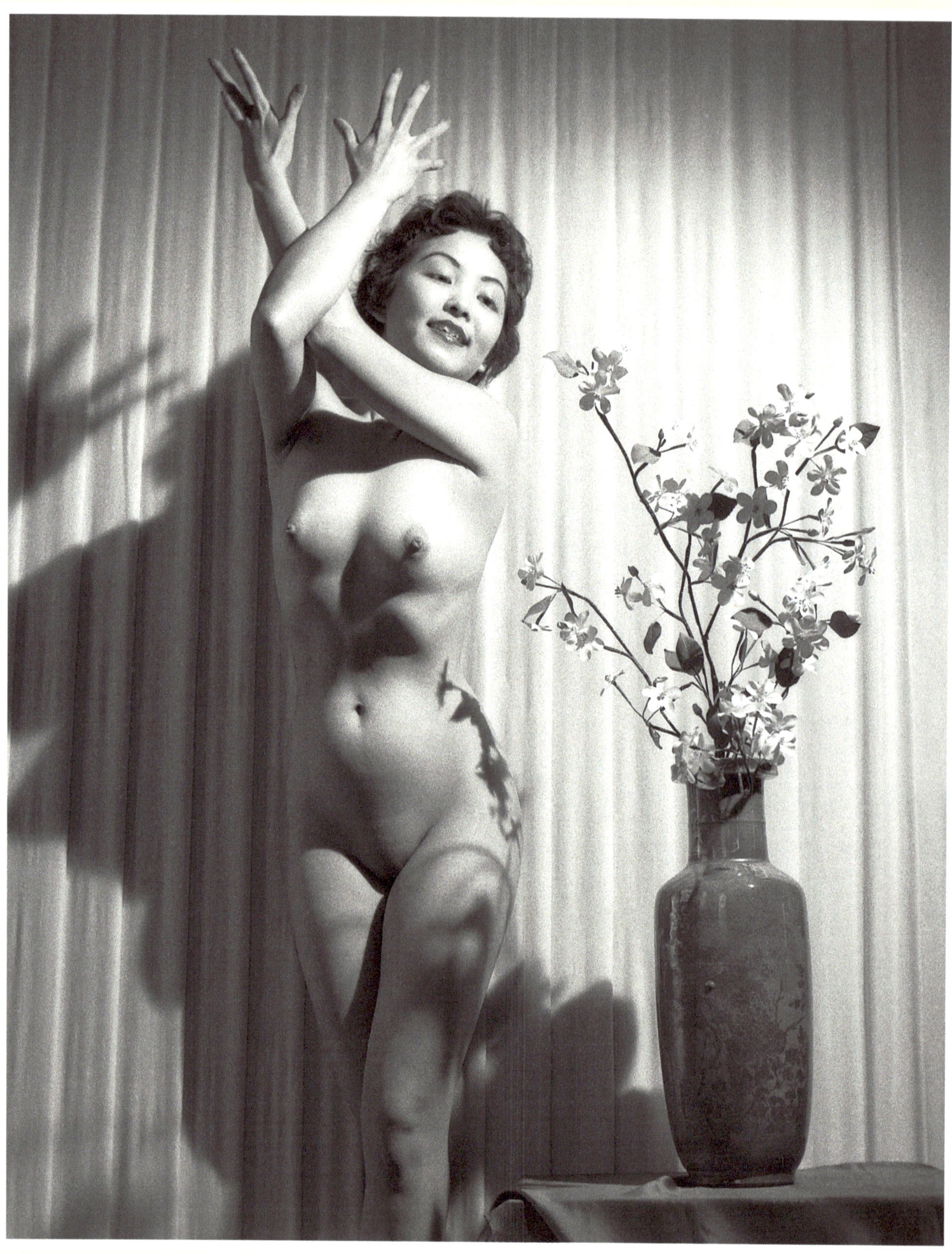

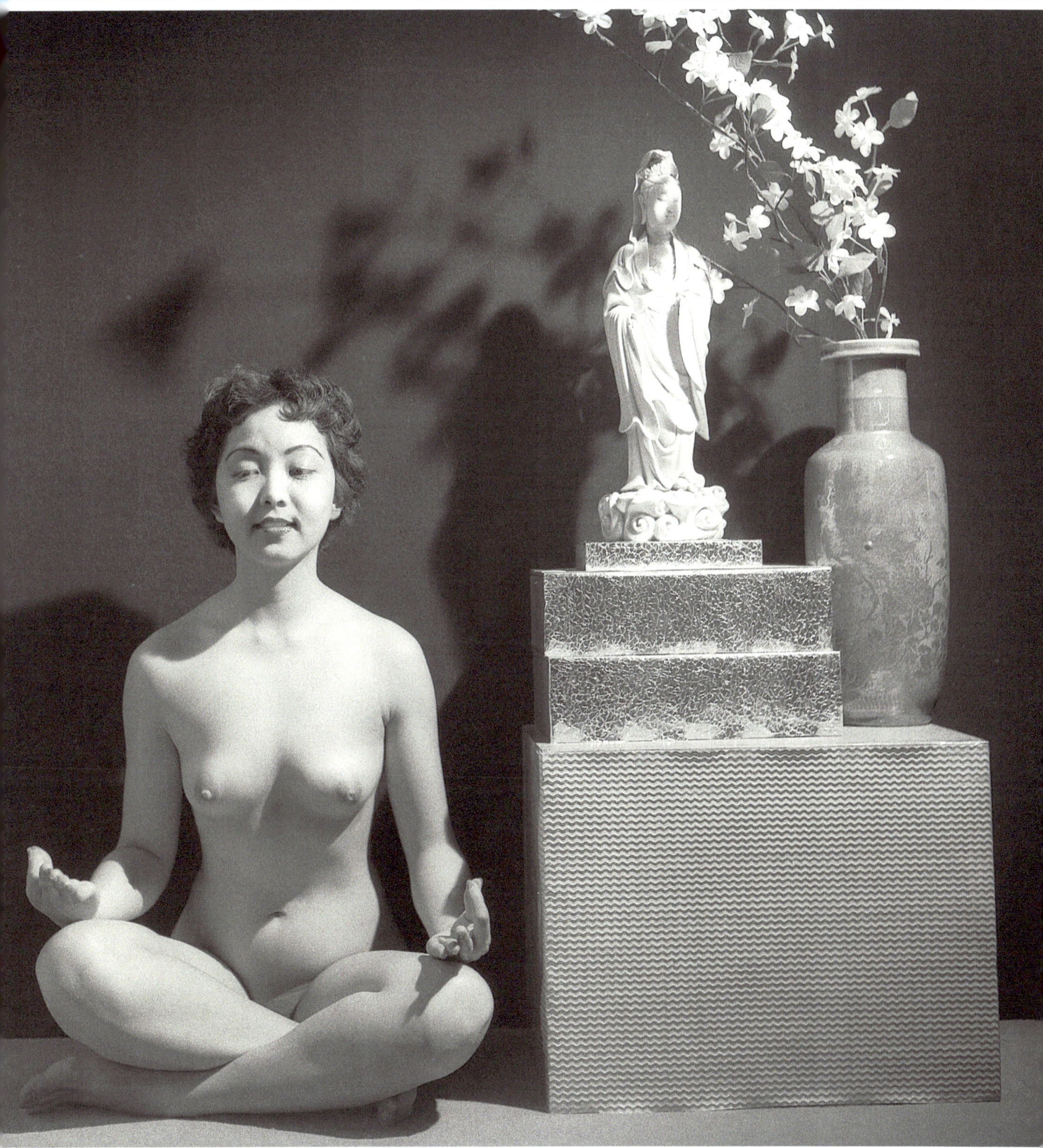

Left and above: Shazi Laine.

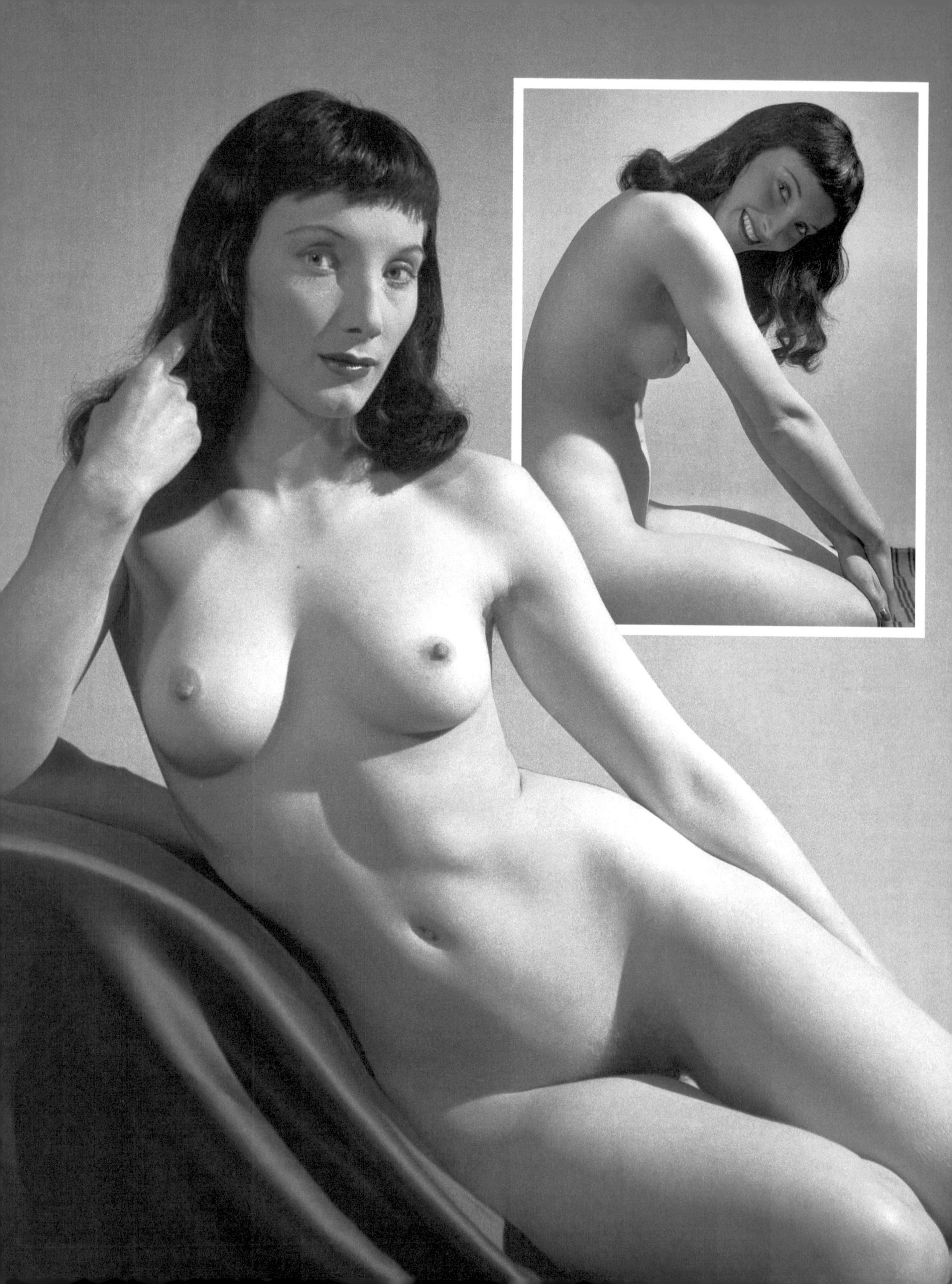

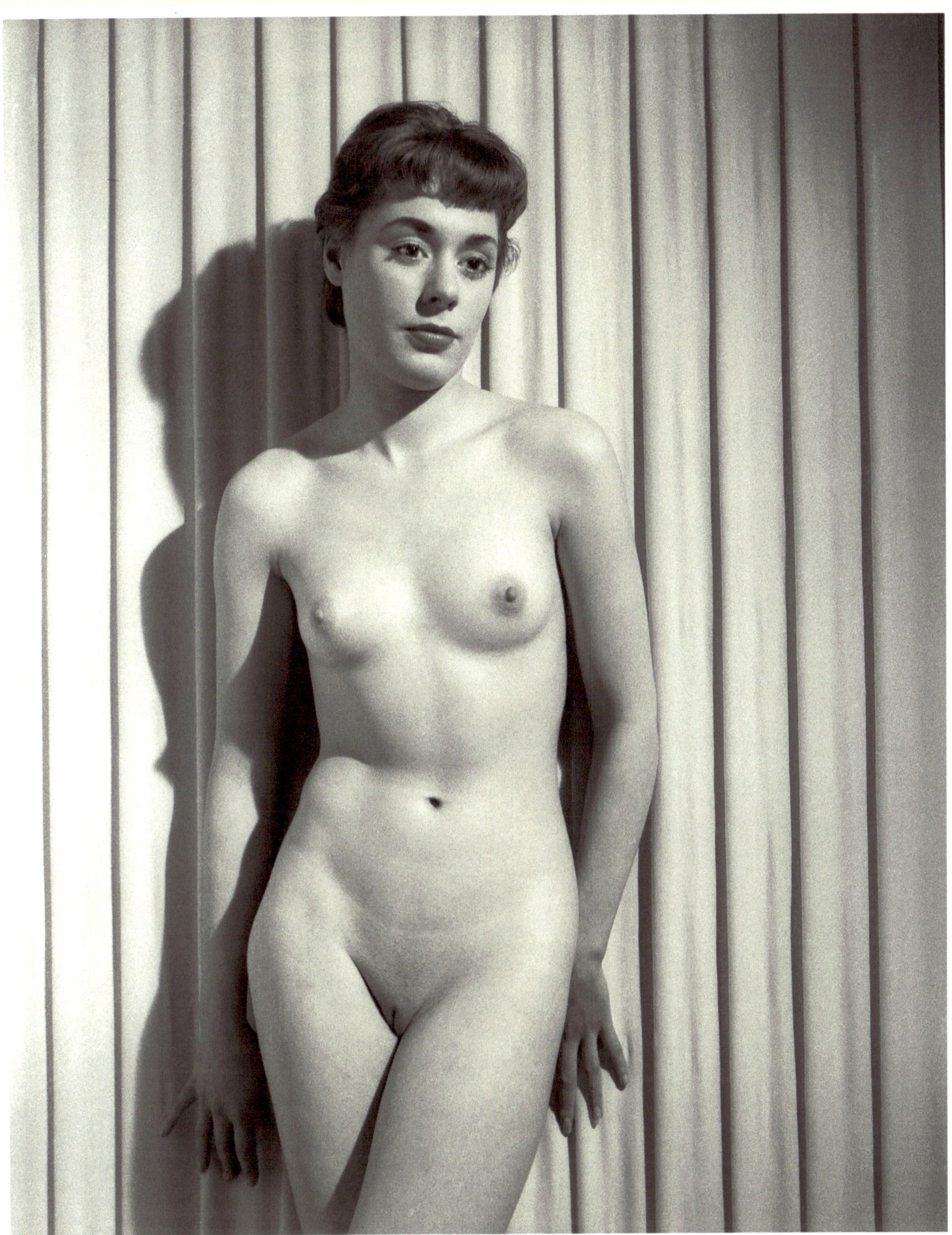

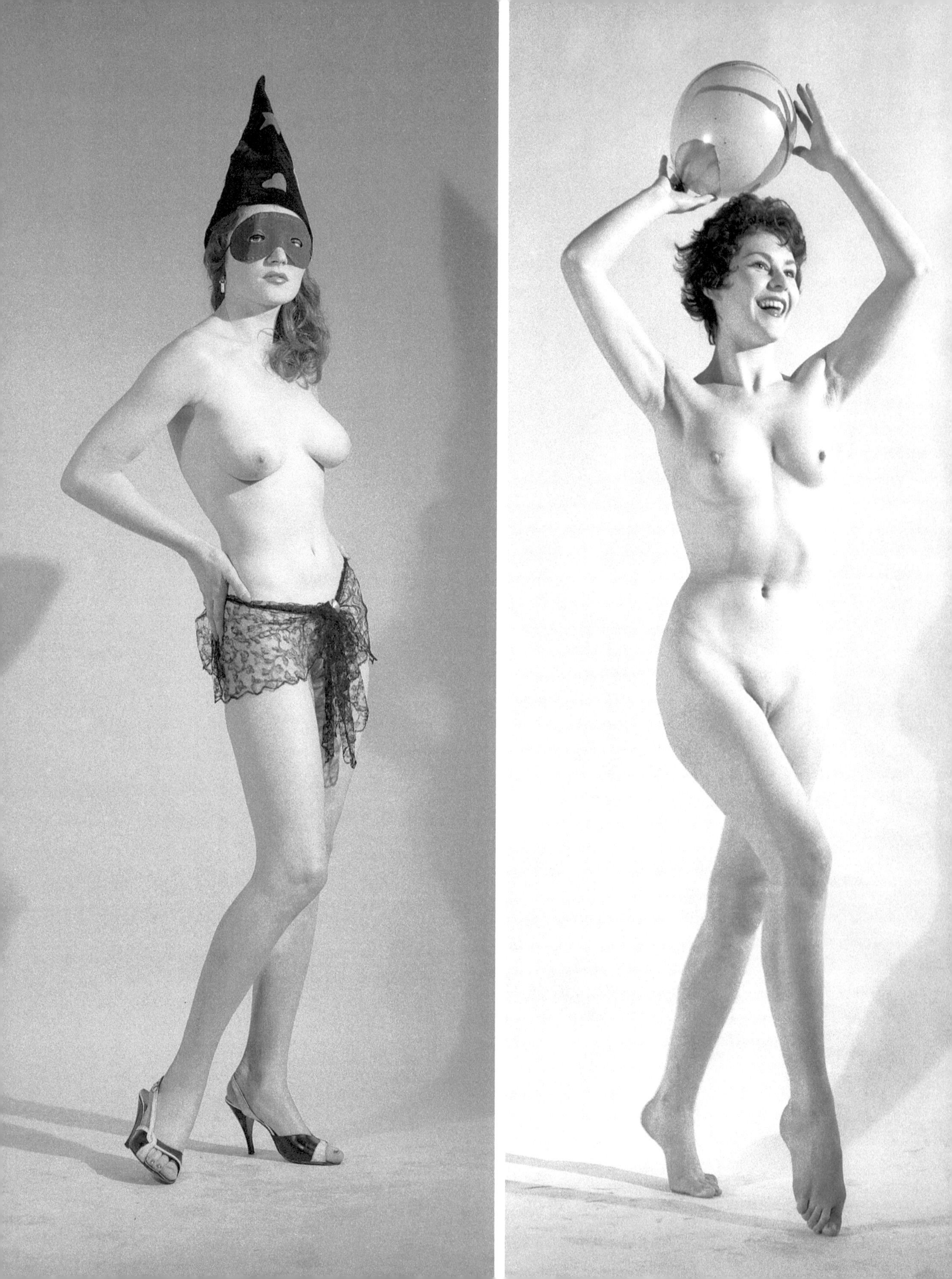

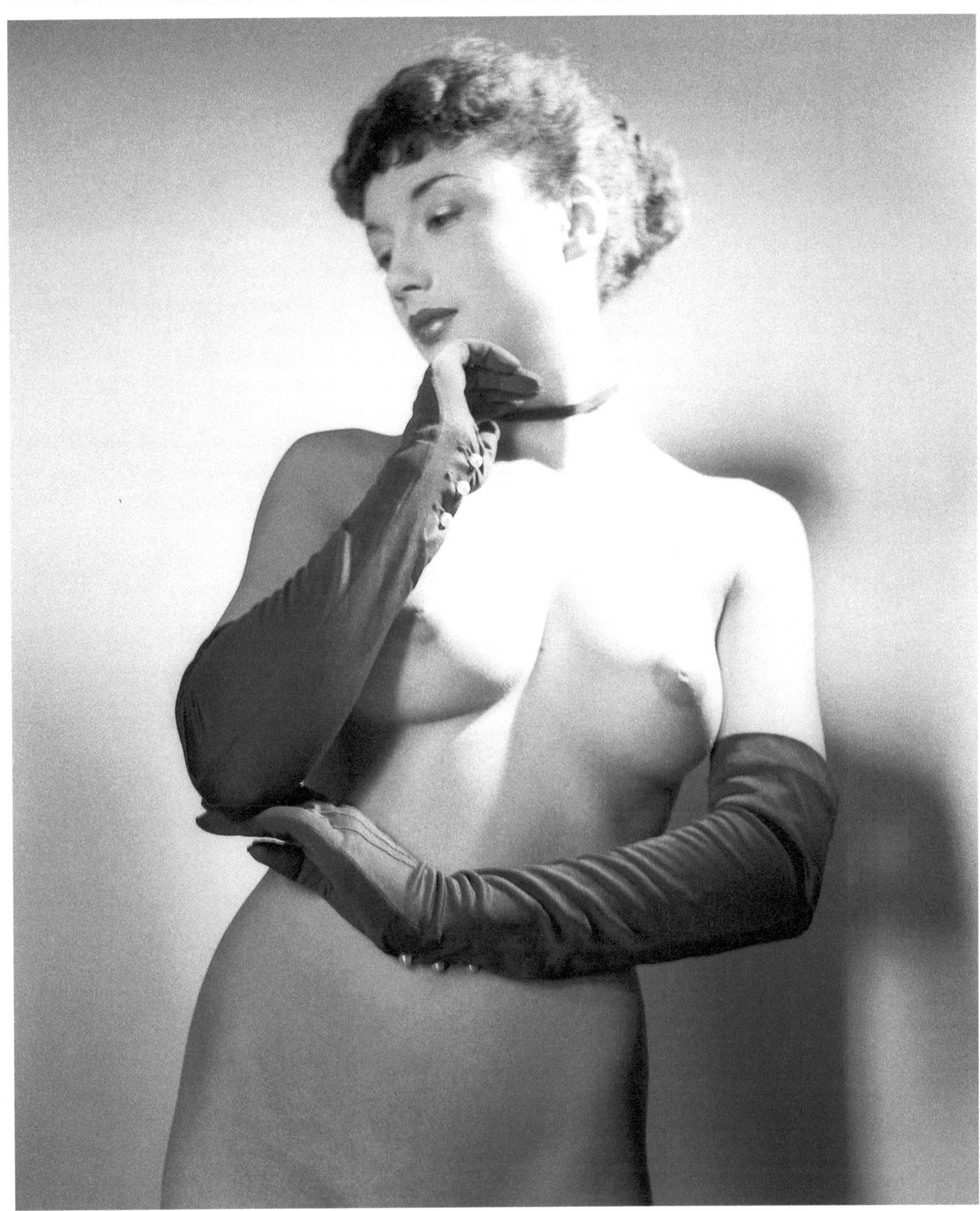

Left: June Russell with a ball. **Above:** the one and only Pamela Green.

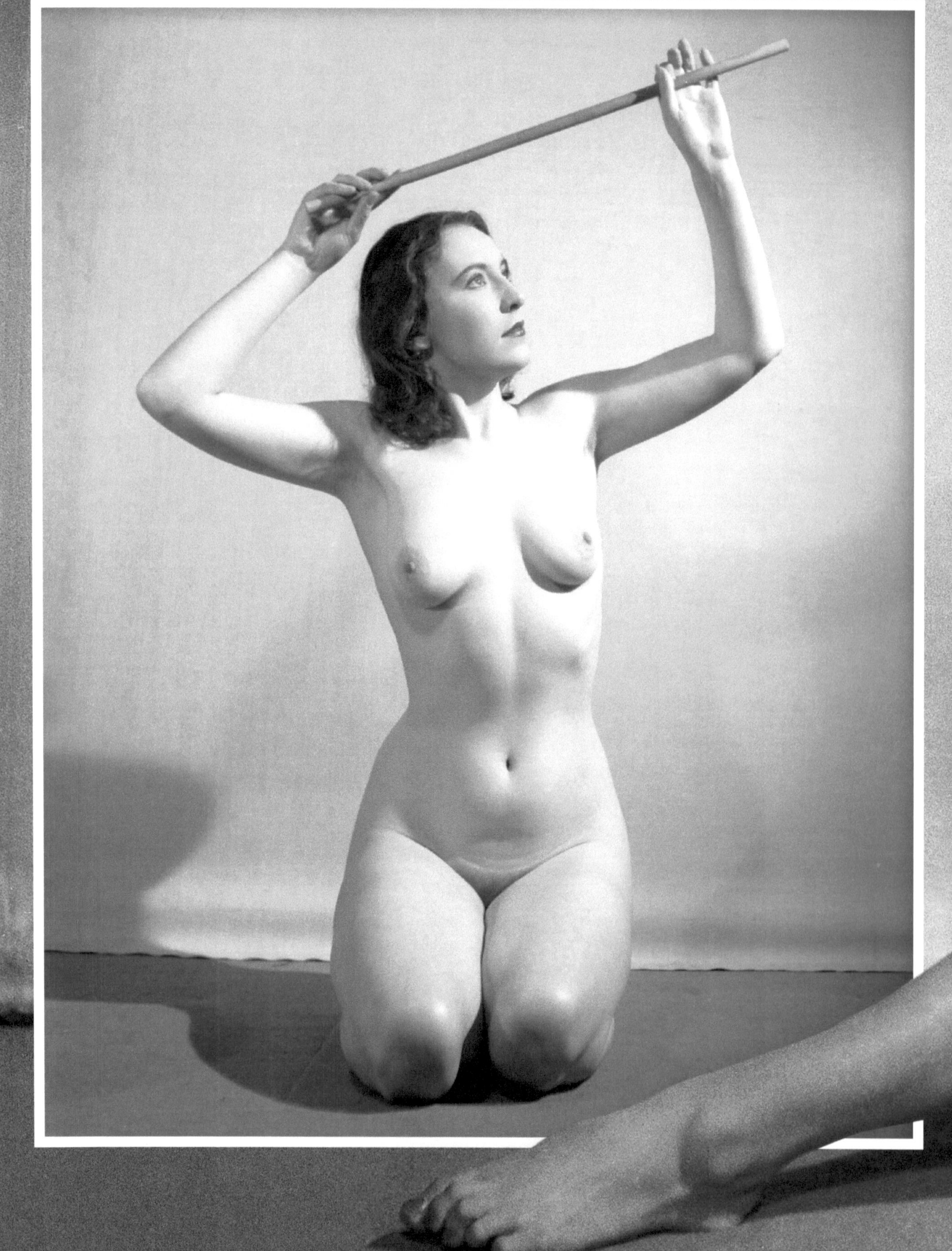

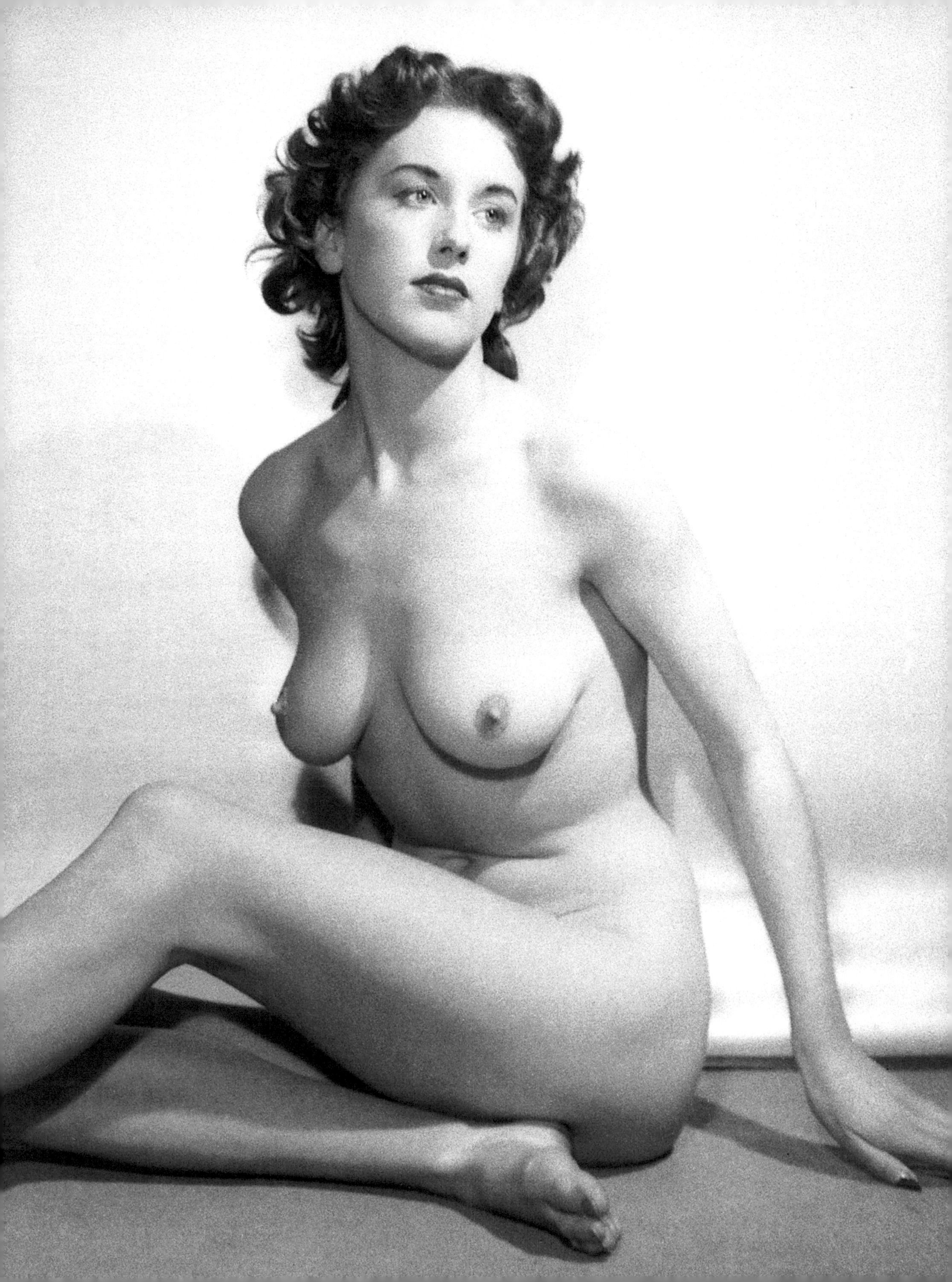

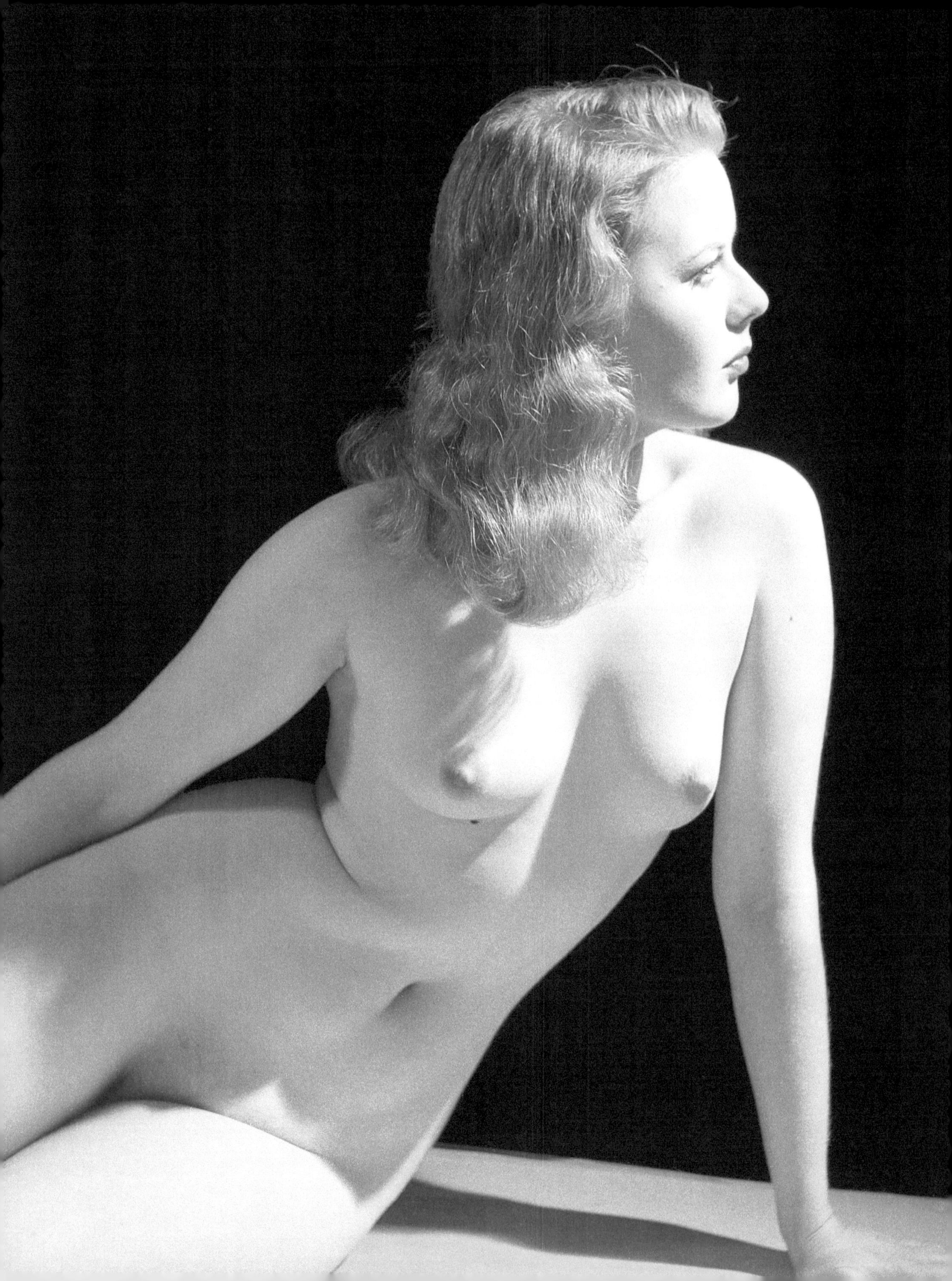

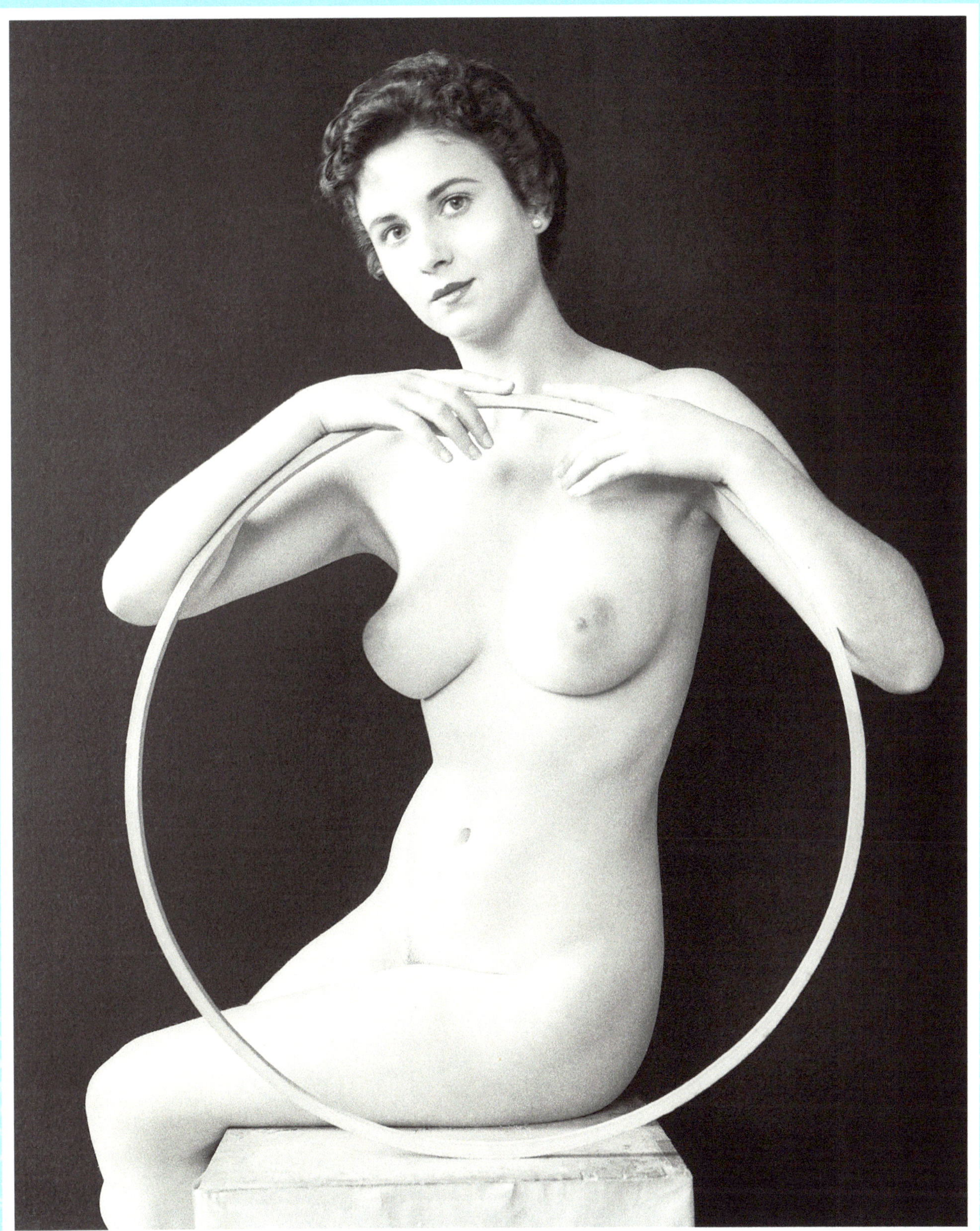

Left: Claudia Gray. Above: Anita Smith, who was photographed by Stephen Glass on numerous occasions.

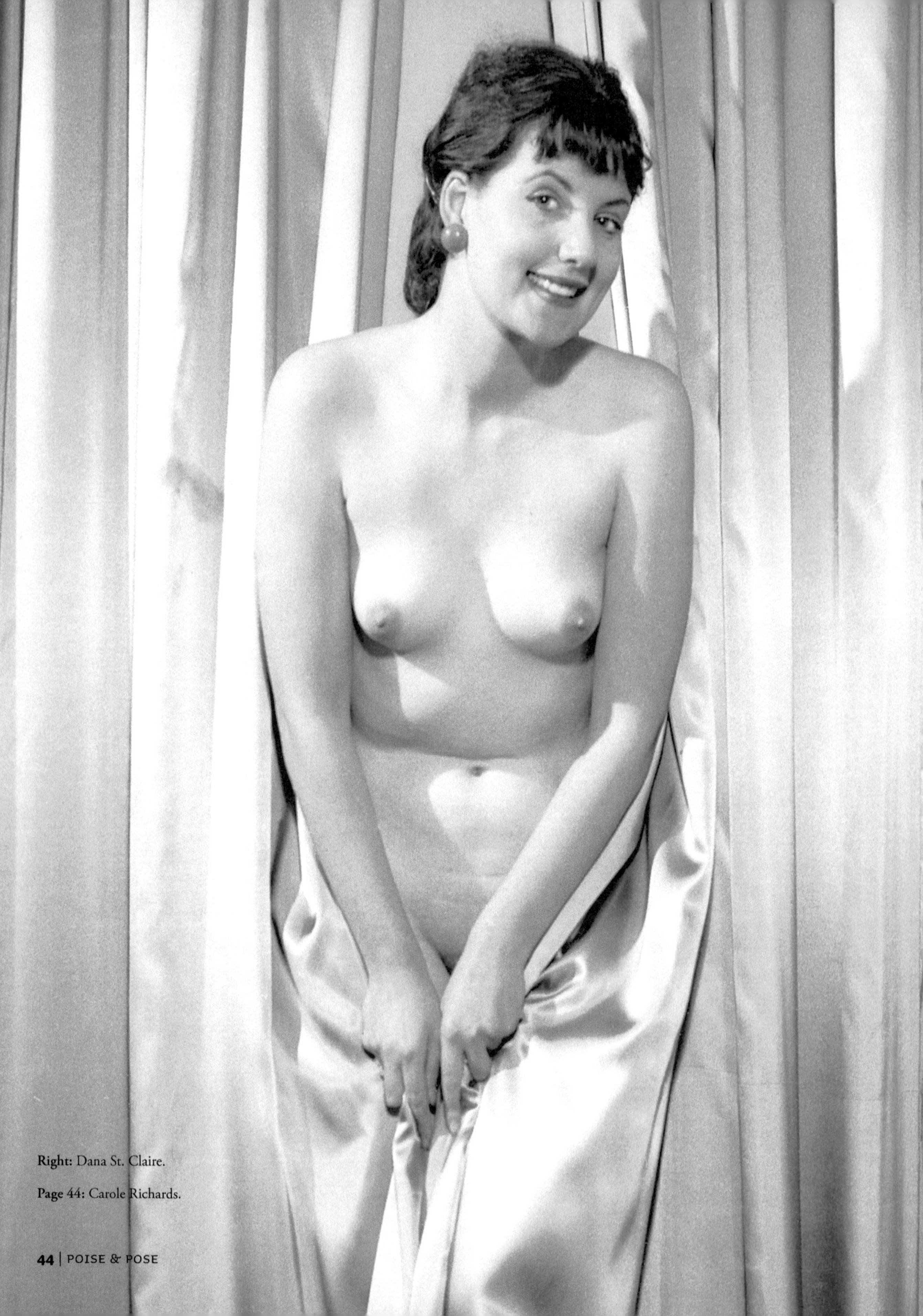

Right: Dana St. Claire.

Page 44: Carole Richards.

ALSO AVAILABLE FROM WOLFBAIT

Doing Rude Things
The history of the British sex film.

Cinema au Naturel
NEW!

A history of nudist film.

Miniten: Rules of the Game
Invented in the 1930s, Miniten is a
tennis-like game played by naturists.

Naked as Nature Intended
The epic tale of a nudist picture by Pamela Green,
with photographs by Douglas "Dambuster" Webb, DFM.

The Naked Truth About Harrison Marks
The notorious biography by Franklyn Wood.

Past Masters of the Nude
An illustrated bibliography of nude photography
books published in England from 1896 to 1960.

THE STEPHEN GLASS COLLECTION

Amazons of Yesteryear
A rare, action-packed collection of images of
wrestling women of the 1940s and 1950s.

Beauty Off-Duty
Relaxed, everyday moments caught on camera.

Naked in the Menagerie
A playful look at Eve accompanied by her animal friends.

Nudist Camp Follies – volumes 1 and 2
An intimate look at the natural
and free atmosphere in Sun Clubs.

Nymphs and Naiads
Beauty unadorned and outdoors.

Poise and Pose
NEW!

A magnificent series of photographs
of female beauty taken in the studio.

Order online at wolfbait.co.uk

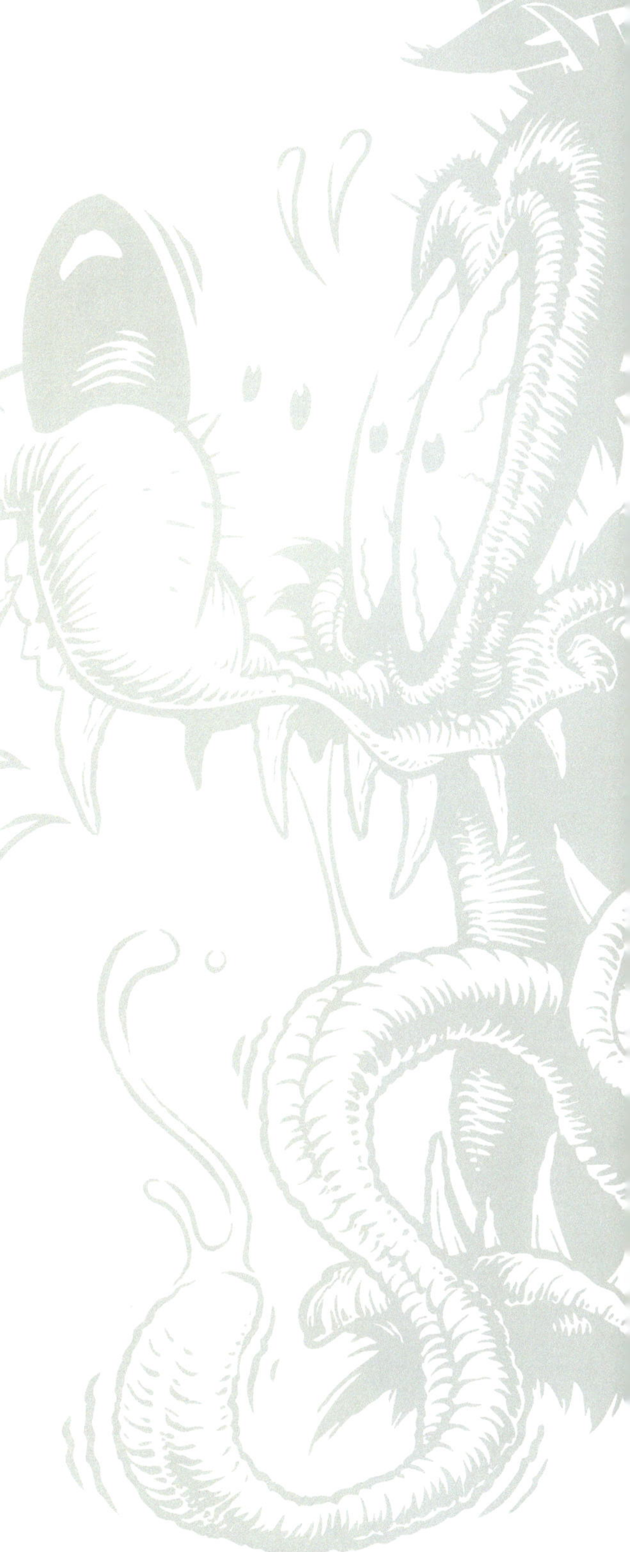

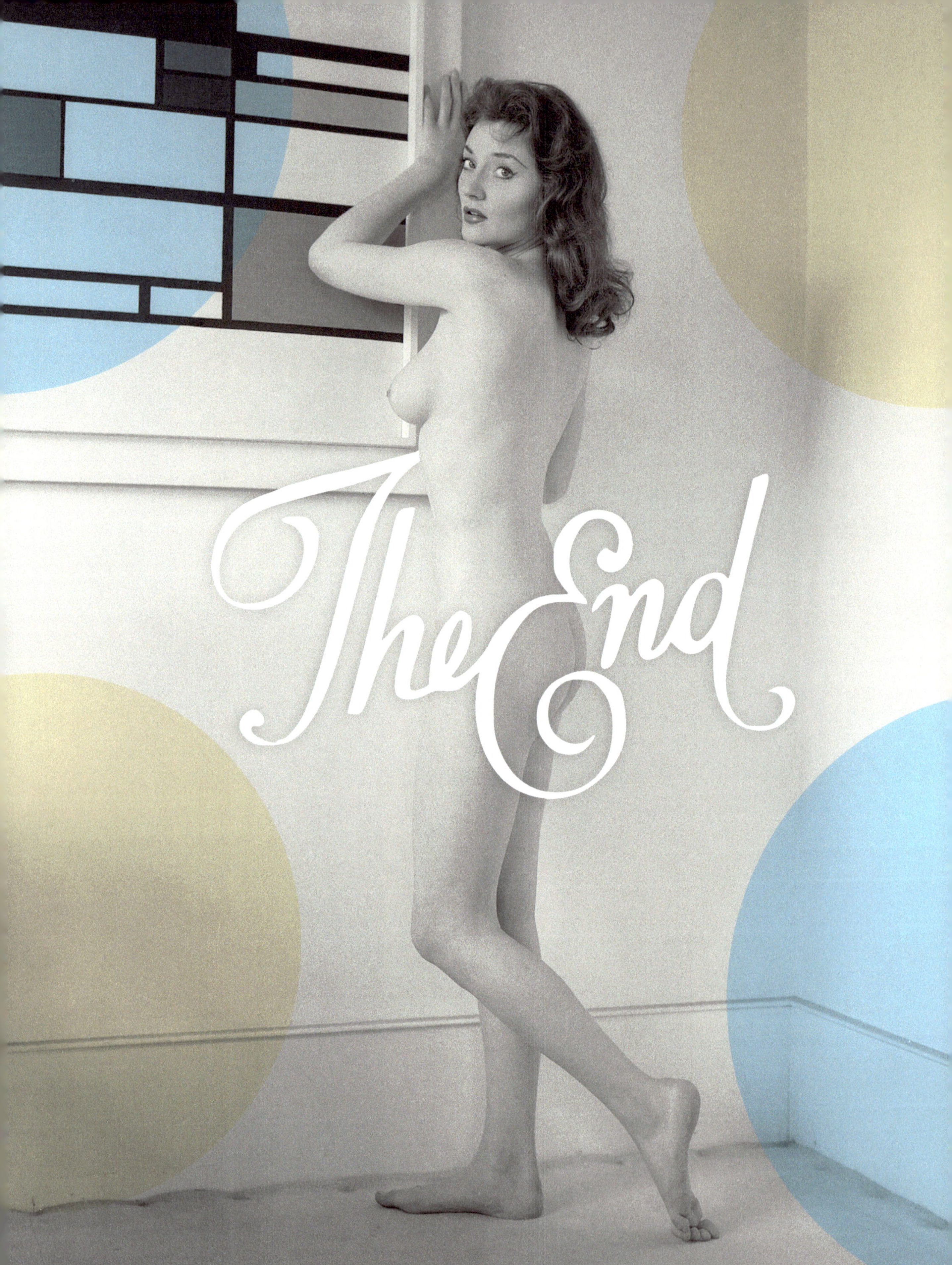
The End